Low-Fat CHICKEN BREASTS

Low-Fat

CHICKEN BREASTS

120 Healthy and Delicious Recipes for Skinless, Boneless Chicken Breasts

·DIANE ROZAS·

A Particular Palate Cookbook ™

THREE RIVERS PRESS
NEW YORK

To Kevin, for his support.

Thanks to Karen Schafer for coordinating and Joan Nielsen for testing.

Published by Three Rivers Press, a division of Crown Publishers, Inc, 201 East 50th Street, New York, New York 10022.
Member of the Crown Publishing Group.

Random House, Inc. New York, Toronto, London, Sydney, Auckland
http://www.randomhouse.com/

Printed in the United States of America

Library of Congress Cataloging-in-Publication Data
Rozas, Diane.
Low-fat chicken breasts: 120 healthy and delicious recipes for skinless, boneless chicken breasts/ by Diane Rozas.
p. cm.
1. Cookery (Chicken). 2. Low-fat diet—Recipes. I. Title.
TX750.5.C45R67 1996
641.6'6—dc20 96-4101
CIP

ISBN 0-517-88634-0

Contents

Introduction 7

Re-Introduction 8

Advice from the Butcher 9

Nutritional Breakdowns 11

Ingredients 12

Techniques 19

Tools 20

Recipes for All Occasions 21

Poach 25

Bake & Roast 51

Sauté 73

Stir-Fry 95

Steam 106

Grill, Broil & Smoke 119

Stove Top 146

Index 174

Introduction

Why choose skinless, boneless chicken breasts to be your next low-fat meal? Simple! Because the breast of the chicken is lower in fat than any other cut of meat and with the skin removed, the breast is one of the best sources of low-fat protein you can find. What's more, there's a difference in fat content between fryer and free-range chicken breasts, the latter boasting even greater leanness.

No matter which you take into your kitchen, the absolute first step to culinary mastery over nature's perfect low-fat food is the recipe. So, instead of searching dozens of books and magazines for a few appealing reduced-fat recipes for chicken breasts, just pick any page in this book. The work has already been done for you.

This is a fresh look at making the chicken breast absolutely delicious, and absolutely low fat in 120 different ways —all without sacrificing our favorite cooking styles, ingredients, or flavor combinations.

The techniques and tools used in these recipes are familiar and easy. In combination with a few tricks of the low-fat cooking trade, such as cooking with nonstick pans and spraying surfaces with vegetable oil cooking spray before cooking, fat is eliminated without losing any flavor, delicacy, tenderness, or taste.

If some of the ingredients lists seem a little longer than usual, it's all in the name of great taste. Complex flavors replace fat flavors, and are created with familiar and innovative ingredient combinations. And though these recipes require much smaller amounts of fats and oils than you might be used to cooking with, they taste as rich and robust as any recipe laden with larger amounts of butter, cream, and oil. Thanks to the efforts of the dairy industry, there are many great-tasting low-fat and nonfat versions of dairy products, including sour cream and yogurt, which allow dishes to be rich and creamy, but not a threat to your health.

Cooking "low fat" is a challenge. You will probably add a few new staples to your kitchen, such as infused oils and vinegars to the pantry, some nonstick skillets to the pot rack, little containers of stock to the freezer, and vegetables and herbs galore to the fridge. These are important steps in the right direction—toward cooking that is not only more healthful but also more flavorful, interesting, and delicious.

One thing I have consistently noticed. If I tell people they are eating a low-fat dish, they immediately begin to feel deprived or cheated. Something is missing. So, I explain that I'm working with some new flavor combinations or exploring a new cooking technique. Or, better yet, I say I just got a new cookbook and I'm trying out a recipe on them. I never say, "This is a really low-fat chicken breast recipe!" Well, maybe I'll spill the secret over after-dinner coffee. They usually don't believe me anyway.

Re-Introduction

Chicken Breasts: *New and Classic Recipes for the Fairest Part of the Fowl,* 1985

More Chicken Breasts: *More New and Classic Recipes for the Fairest Part of the Fowl,* 1991

This book, *Low-Fat Chicken Breasts,* is the third in a series on preparing and cooking chicken breasts. Over the past ten years, I've become the champion of chicken breasts, and have eaten and cooked much more than my share of this lean white meat. And still, I love it and proudly serve it to anyone who will join me at my table.

I have long thought of the chicken breast as the perfect food. In the early part of the 1980s it was my staple. I had virtually hundreds of recipes, and used to make Xerox copies of them and pass them out at work. Even then, people I had never met would call me for recipes. Finally, I thought it would be easier to direct my callers to a bookstore than to go home every night and try to match up chicken breast recipes with the tastes of people I had never met.

After months of writing, testing, and editing, I experienced the thrill of ushering my cookbook, *Chicken Breasts,* into the world in1985. As it quickly sold out its first printing (much to the amazement of the publisher), it was reprinted (nervously), only to sell out again. So, it was reprinted again and again and again. Finally, when it hit ten printings, I was able to sit back and say (to myself, of course), "I suppose people really do like chicken breast dishes as much as I do."

But that was then, and this is now, and there is more to be said on the subject of preparing, cooking, and serving chicken breasts.

I had begun to address the low-fat

issue in my second book, *More Chicken Breasts,* but in a fanciful way. It has a "Spa" recipe section and the idea behind the "Grazing" section is a chic way to control portions. And the book's "Salads" section offers some delicious low-fat recipes with light vinaigrettes.

After the release of *More Chicken Breasts* in 1991, my files began to expand and overflow with recipes of a different nature: low in fat and calories and highly flavored. And, yes, many of them were for chicken breasts.

Recently, I fancied writing an article on elegant, low-fat chicken breast recipes for entertaining, dishes that would grace the finest tables and look delicious on the prettiest china. Then I got into a barbecuing mood, and a few dozen new ideas popped into my mind; meanwhile, dozens of sautéing recipes fell out of my files. It was déjà vu: In front of me were a ton of chicken breast recipes, every one a low-fat beauty. It seemed as though another book was the way to go.

In this book the focus is both low fat and intense flavor: light, fresh fare made with lots of herbs and spices, replacing high-fat ingredients with concentrated flavor combinations. I hope you will collect all three cookbooks and use them often.

Advice from the Butcher

The right way to buy, store, skin, bone, split, and flatten chicken breasts

THE CHICKEN BREAST

Specifics

- One breast is usually divided or split into two halves. Each half equals one serving, and weighs 6 to 8 ounces.
- A 6.5-ounce skinless, boneless piece of chicken breast (an average half-breast serving) contains 197 calories and 6.5 grams of fat.
- Prices range from $2 to $6 per pound. Frozen breasts are least expensive; fresh free-range chicken is most expensive.
- It's best to buy fresh chicken breasts and use them within 1 day. Slowly thaw frozen breasts in the refrigerator before using. Remember, never thaw frozen poultry at room temperature.

Note on Chicken Breast "Fillets" or "Tenders": They have become a popular part of the chicken breast since they started being packaged separately. The fillet, or tender, is the part of the breast that is located on the underside. These pieces must be trimmed before they are used in cooking (see page 11 for instructions in removing the tendon), and can be used as appetizers, in such dishes as fajitas or salads, or whenever you want to prepare bite-size pieces of chicken breast.

Note on Fat Calories: Half the fat and calories of the chicken breast is in the skin, so remove it before cooking. If you like to keep the skin on during broiling, grilling, or roasting to keep the breast meat moist, peel it off while the chicken breasts are still hot and discard.

Note on Doneness: Chicken should never be served rare. The internal temperature of doneness for a boneless breast is 160° F., or when the juices run clear or slightly yellow, but never pink. To make sure, cut one of the breasts open through the center before removing from the heat.

BUYING AND STORING CHICKEN BREASTS

Buy only the freshest chicken breasts for immediate use. Check the date on the package, or use the old-fashioned, no-fail smell test. A less-than-fresh chicken breast cannot conceal its age! Look for plump, bruise-free meat. The color is meaningless; it varies depending on chicken feeds used throughout the country. Immediately refrigerate the meat when you get it home. If you're not cooking the breasts within 1 or 2 days, wrap each breast tightly in several layers of plastic wrap, or place in individual plastic sandwich bags to keep them from drying out. Freeze them if you are not cooking by the day before the package expiration date.

Note on Health and Safety: Remember, chicken breasts are susceptible to salmonella bacteria. Raw chicken should not come in contact with other foods. Always wash the work surfaces, cutting boards, knives, and other utensils with hot soapy water after preparing raw breast meat. Wash your hands as well. Never refreeze frozen chicken that has been thawed. If you are marinating the chicken, discard any marinade that was not cooked along with the chicken. Never store it for reuse.

BONING AND SKINNING CHICKEN BREASTS

You can save several dollars per pound if you skin and bone chicken breasts at home rather than buy prepackaged or butcher-skinned and -boned chicken breasts. Because the bone and skin act as a natural casing, freshly boned and skinned chicken breasts may remain more moist, fresh, and succulent when prepared just prior to cooking. Once you have a little practice, boning and skinning is a simple process that takes only a few minutes. Freezing the chicken breasts for half an hour before beginning makes the meat firmer and the process even easier.

Skinning: Place the breast on a work surface, skin side up. With your fingers, peel the skin back and off. Trim away any remaining bits of skin and fat with a sharp knife.

Boning

1. Use a very sharp boning knife with a flexible blade. Insert the tip at one end of the breastbone, between the rib cage and the meat, keeping the knife as close as possible to the rib cage. Work the tip along the edge of the breast from one end to the other, running the knife right along the ribs. Separate the meat from the bone to the depth of 2 inches. (At this point the breast meat will still be attached in the center to the breastbone on both sides.)

2. With the knife and your fingers, scrape or push the meat toward the breastbone until it is completely loosened from the rib cage but still attached to the breastbone.

3. Scrape and push the meat away from the breastbone, being careful not to tear the meat. Remove the breast meat.

SPLITTING THE CHICKEN BREAST AND REMOVING THE TENDON

1. Using your sharp boning knife, slice the breast in half following the center indentation, where it was attached to the bone. Slice on either side of the cartilage and discard the hard white cartilage that separated the breasts.

2. Slip the point of the boning knife under one end of the white tendon running along the underside of the breast and lift the tendon away from the meat. Hold an end of the tendon with one hand while lifting and scraping the meat away carefully. Trim off any bits of fat or skin.

FLATTENING CHICKEN BREASTS

Use a flat-headed metal pounder or wooden mallet to flatten chicken breasts to a uniform thickness. First place the breasts, skinned side up, between two sheets of plastic wrap and gently pound to the required thickness with light, even strokes. The heel of the palm or the bottom of a heavy skillet are also good flattening devices.

Nutritional Breakdowns

THE REAL SKINNY ON FAT GRAMS

The USDA recommendation of 30 percent maximum fat in the diet is an overall figure—not a per meal, per dish, or per item ratio, but rather a total figure of your entire intake, and the figures are calculated over a three-day period! The way one calculates fat in foods is, at this stage, fairly standardized, but it takes a nutrition specialist to create a personal program that gives you the exact percentages that are right for you.

Though all of the recipes in this book

have only 30 percent or less of their calories derived from fat, they are meant to be integrated into an overall healthful and varied diet. You may eat something that is slightly higher in fat, and another dish that is lower in fat; all you need to remember is that you should reach a reasonable balance in the end. If the recipe says it serves 4 to 6, the nutritional analysis pertains to the smaller number of servings.

Ingredients

Important things to keep in your freezer, add to the pantry, and have on hand in the fridge

BUTTER, OILS, AND COOKING SPRAY

Butter: Use only unsalted (sweet) butter to avoid adding extra salt where it is not required.

A Variety of Oils: Experiment with several until you find a brand of olive oil that you like. (Extra-virgin or virgin olive oil can be used for cooking, although extra-virgin is the more intensely flavored of the two.) Canola is another good basic unsaturated cooking oil. Choose corn, peanut, clear sesame, and grapeseed oil more often than any nonspecific "vegetable" oil. Oils should be very fresh. Never reuse previously used oils.

Infused Oils: Infused oils are a great way to add flavor. To prepare, place the ingredients in a glass jar and cover with 1 to 4 cups of extra-virgin olive oil. Cover tightly and allow to marinate a few days in the refrigerator before straining and using. Try any of these combinations: rosemary and garlic; thyme and bay leaves; peppercorns and oregano sprigs; porcini mushrooms and pink peppercorns; a few slivers of truffle; citrus zests; or just garlic cloves. For best results, store these oils in the refrigerator.

Vegetable Oil Cooking Spray: Vegetable oil cooking spray is readily called for throughout this book. Primarily, it allows cooks to decrease the amount of oil needed to prevent food from sticking to the pan. It is often used when sautéing and grilling. Try to find the pure and unflavored kind. If you have a can on the shelf and can't remember when you bought it, invest in a new can, please!

BREAD CRUMB AND CRUST COMBINATIONS

Make your own low-fat or nonfat crumbs and coatings with melba toast, cornflakes or other low-fat breakfast flakes, any yeast bread, calorie-reduced breads, and cornmeal. Make fresh or dried bread crumbs in a food processor fitted with the metal blade. Add dried seasonings, or ground spices, citrus zests, pepper, and salt, as desired. Store in the refrigerator or freezer. Create flavor combinations that complement or intensify the predominant flavor in the recipe.

LOW-FAT AND NONFAT DAIRY PRODUCTS

Sour cream now comes in both low-fat and fat-free versions, as does mayonnaise. All of these new and improved products have slight differences in taste and textures. It's best to do a taste test to find your favorite.

Low- and no-fat yogurts have been available for a long time and are also delicious. Low-fat and nonfat cream cheese can be used successfully, in smaller quantities, to thicken sauces, and 1 percent milk or nonfat milk can be substituted easily for whole milk. Low-fat cheeses have improved in texture and flavor, although they may need more time to melt than regular cheeses. Fat-free cheeses are not recommended for cooking. However, very finely grated hard, aged cheeses like pecorino Romano and Parmesan provide big flavor in small amounts. All these and other reduced-fat dairy products are readily available in supermarkets and health food stores.

HERBS, SPICES, AND AROMATICS

Certain herbs and spices work especially well with chicken breasts and by altering the seasonings of the recipe you can create new versions. Try to use fresh herbs whenever called for in the recipe. But there are times when it's dried or nothing, so be sure to replenish your dried herb supply at least every six months because the flavors lose their potency very quickly. As a rule of thumb (if one is possible since the strength of herbs varies so much), use just one third the amount of dried as fresh.

Herbs: Be prepared for any recipe with a supply of fresh and dried herbs, including flat-leaf parsley, basil, tarragon, chervil, marjoram, thyme, bay leaf, fresh ginger, and cilantro.

Spices and Seasonings: Keep on hand: curry powder, dried red pepper flakes or whole chilies, peppercorns, kosher salt, coriander seed, dry mustard, and allspice berries. A pepper mill should be used any time freshly ground black or white pepper is called for in a recipe.

Aromatics: These members of the lily family add depth of flavor to recipes; their flavor intensity depends on the type of aromatic, the cooking method, and time. A whole fresh head of garlic is a must-have staple. Shallots, with their mild onion taste, add a flavor dimension that is well suited to the quick-cooking chicken breast. Many longer-cooking and ethnic flavored dishes instead require white or yellow onions. Try cooking with the sweet onion family. New crops are popping up in Florida, though Maui, Vidalia, and Walla Walla are the best known of the sweets. Also keep green onions, or scallions, on hand.

LOW-FAT PANTRY REGULARS

These ingredients appear frequently in this collection of low-fat recipes, and many boast an especially high concentration of flavor with relatively low fat and calories when used in moderation. Keep these in your pantry or refrigerator and a wonderful chicken breast dinner will always be at your fingertips: a tin of anchovies; dried ancho chilies; a can of green chilies; a can of chipotle chilies in adobo sauce; oil-cured Niçoise and Kalamata olives; tree-ripened olives from California; canned or boxed cooked crushed tomatoes; sun-dried tomatoes (dry-packed); tamari and reduced-sodium soy sauce; Asian fish sauce; hoisin; vinegars: balsamic, white, white wine, rice wine, sherry, herb- and fruit-infused vinegars; and a selection of oils (see page 12 for suggestions).

WINES AND LIQUORS

The clear, dry characteristics of good white wine, especially Chardonnay, are almost always a match with chicken breasts (although certain recipe ingredients, like artichokes, can put a damper on the taste of any wine). Other drier and slightly stronger-tasting whites, such as Sauvignon Blanc, are great substitutions for Chardonnay in many of the recipes.

Besides a sampling of white wines, consider the following for splashes of high flavor, especially for sautés and sauces: a bottle of good Cognac, Champagne, dry and medium sherry, dry vermouth, dark rum, Grand Marnier, and port or Madeira.

Light red wines, like California Pinot Noir, Italian Dolcetto, and French Beaujolais, are perfect for more complex, earthier chicken breast dishes. Sweet late-harvest wines and most full-bodied red wines are overwhelming to this delicate part of the chicken. Ultimately, it's a matter of taste.

Good-quality wine is recommended for both cooking and drinking. The rule: If you can enjoy a glass of it, then it deserves to be an ingredient in the dish you are making. Avoid buying supermarket wines labeled "cooking wine," which are for the most part poor in quality and undrinkable.

MARINADES—WET AND DRY

These are not to be confused with barbecue sauces. They are flavor-enhancing combinations of spices and herbs or other ingredients such as minced onion or garlic. Some contain liquids and oil and are applied wet; others are applied dry and contain no liquids. Rubbed onto the chicken breast, dry marinades usually have more ground spices and herbs mixed with just a little bit of oil. When using a dry marinade to roast, grill, or broil chicken breasts there is no need to add any other oil to the recipe. Chicken breasts absorb the flavors of wet marinades in 1 to 2 hours. Lightly pat dry before adding to the hot pan.

PUREES

Low-fat recipes often require a bit more preparation to get the flavor balance going. Like marinade, concentrated herb and vegetable purees have that magical ability to enhance a recipe with intense flavors and can be totally fat free.

What to Puree: Roasted red, yellow, or orange peppers; oven-roasted garlic; roasted onions (red and yellow); raw or steamed spinach; herb combinations (such as pestos); and cooked potatoes. Keep herb purees on hand in the refrigerator or freezer—they can be used to enhance many different recipes and create new ones. A highly flavored wine and herb stock (see the recipe on pages 16–17) can be flavored and thickened with purees to make an elegant, fat-free sauce.

Thickeners: Use a puree of cooked potato to create a sauce with body. Go ahead, experiment with white, or even sweet potatoes, or red yams. Things could get very interesting in your kitchen!

SIMPLE CHICKEN STOCK

This following stock recipe is perfect for all the recipes in this book calling for chicken stock. If you decide to use canned stock, choose a low-sodium, defatted brand.

2 pounds chicken parts, including necks and backs

6 cups cold water, or more as needed

1 stalk celery, coarsely chopped, leaf included

1 carrot, peeled and quartered

1 onion (skin on), root end trimmed

1 leek, cleaned and coarsely chopped

Bouquet garni (see page 18), containing flat-leaf parsley, bay leaf, fresh thyme sprigs, peppercorns, and cloves (optional)

1. In a 4- to 6-quart nonaluminum stockpot, combine the chicken parts and enough cold water to cover. Slowly bring just to a boil, over medium heat, and then immediately reduce the heat and simmer for 45 minutes. Remember, do not boil stock! Frequently skim off the foam that collects on the surface until there is no more scum. (A well-skimmed stock will be clear when chilled; a murky and cloudy broth will result if it hasn't been skimmed very well or if the stock is boiled.)

2. Add the celery, carrot, onion, leek, bouquet garni, and more water to cover the ingredients completely, if necessary. Simmer over low heat, partially covered, for 2 to 3 hours, or until the stock is very flavorful.

3. Remove the stockpot from the heat. With a slotted spoon, remove and discard the vegetables. Pour the stock through a fine mesh strainer or a colander lined with a double layer of dampened cheesecloth into a clean, nonaluminum pot, pressing the bones and meat to extract all the liquid. Cool the stock to room temperature. Refrigerate, uncovered, for 12 to 24 hours.

4. When thoroughly chilled, remove the layer of yellow fat from the top with a spoon. Refrigerate, covered, for up to 4 days, or freeze in 1- and 2-cup individual containers, or make into stock cubes (see page 18).

RICH CHICKEN STOCK

Rich chicken stock is simple chicken stock (see above recipe) that has been reduced by 50 percent or more. Take 4 cups of stock and simmer, uncovered, until it is reduced to 2 cups, or less. Store rich stock in the freezer in small containers. Use this stock in all the recipes in this book calling for Rich Chicken Stock.

HERB AND WINE STOCK

This stock, called *nage* in French, is a long-cooking, highly aromatic, fat-free vegetable, wine, and herb stock that can be strained and reduced further. It is used as a base for making highly flavored, low- and no-fat sauces, or as a poaching broth. It's very versatile and should be kept frozen for immediate availability. Once prepared, the flavorful *nage* can be thickened with vegetable purees (see page 15), and simply drizzled over a poached chicken breast, or cooked with accompanying ingredients (such as beans, potatoes, pasta, or vegetable ragouts) to create the type of low-fat dish that is especially flavorful.

1½ teaspoons canola or other vegetable oil
1 large yellow onion, chopped
1 large leek, washed and chopped
½ stalk celery, chopped
1 whole head garlic, loose outside papery skin removed, cut in half crosswise
1 large fennel bulb, diced
½ bunch fresh thyme
3 bay leaves
½ bunch flat-leaf parsley
1 bottle (750 ml) dry white wine (preferably Chardonnay)

In a large saucepan, heat the oil. Add the onion, leek, celery, garlic, and fennel, and cook over medium heat just until the vegetables are translucent, but not browned, about 7 minutes. Add the thyme, bay leaves, parsley, and wine. Bring to a boil. Reduce the heat immediately, and simmer for approximately 45 minutes. Add 2 cups of water and bring to a boil. Lower the heat and simmer for another 20 minutes. Being careful not to press down on the vegetables, pour the stock through a fine mesh strainer and discard the vegetables. Chill and reserve in the refrigerator for up to 2 days until ready to cook, or freeze.

NONFAT VEGETABLE STOCK

The quantities in this recipe depend on the size of your stockpot. Basically, a spa veggie stock consists of vegetables, fresh herbs, and bottled water. Use whatever vegetables you like that are available or in season, avoiding vegetables with very pungent flavors, such as cabbage. Make from 6 to 10 cups of stock. You'll use it with good results in many recipes, and it can be substituted for chicken stock. It is a perfect flavorful poaching liquid.

VEGETABLE STOCK

In the proportion of your choice:

Zucchini
Sweet bell peppers (red, yellow, or green)
Turnips
Onions
Celery (no tops)
Carrots
Garlic cloves
Bay leaf
Fresh herbs (such as parsley, lemon basil, thyme, rosemary)
Black peppercorns (10 or more)
Whole cloves
Nutmeg

1. Place all the ingredients in a 6-quart stockpot. Pour on 10 cups of spring or bottled water. Bring to a boil, lower the heat, and cook gently at a slow, low simmer for 1 hour. Do not boil. Add more water as needed to keep the vegetables covered with water throughout the cooking process.
2. Cool to room temperature. Pour the stock through a fine mesh strainer lined with a double layer of dampened cheesecloth. Do not press on the vegetables, and after they are well drained, discard.
3. Store in the refrigerator for up to 1 week or freeze in small amounts (see page 18 for instructions).

Note: Don't use cracked or ground pepper or salt in the stock. Add it later when correcting the seasonings. *Do not reduce this stock, as you would chicken stock, because it becomes bitter.*

DEFATTED CHICKEN STOCK

In most supermarkets and health food stores, cans of reduced-fat and reduced-sodium stock are available. However, you can make your own defatted chicken stock by the following method.

How to: Strain the stock (use the Simple Chicken Stock or Rich Chicken Stock recipe on pages 15–16, or another homemade stock recipe) through a fine mesh strainer to remove all the solids. To use the stock while it is still hot, measure out the amount you need right away. Line the strainer with a layer of cheesecloth and pour the stock through again. Let it sit for a few minutes to allow the remaining fat to rise to the surface. Spoon the fat out carefully from the surface until no more remains on top. Or, place the strained stock in the refrigerator overnight. The layer of fat that collects on top of the stock can be lifted up and removed. Check for fat particles on top of the stock and discard. Place in small containers for future use.

STORING STOCKS AND MAKING STOCK CUBES

Storing: When a recipe calls for a small amount of stock, it's great to have a pure, fat-free ounce or two of your own stock to toss into the mix of ingredients and enhance your cooking endeavors. After the stock chills and all the excess fat, if any, is removed from its surface, divide the stock according to uses in 1- and 2-cup containers and freeze, or make stock cubes.

Making Stock Cubes: Reduce some of the stock to about one quarter of the original amount, pour it into ice cube trays, and freeze. Transfer the frozen cubes to plastic Ziploc freezer bags.

BOUQUET GARNI

This classic French combination of fresh herbs, spices, and other highly flavored ingredients is used to infuse flavor into stocks. It usually contains bay leaf, parsley, thyme, leek, and black peppercorns. You can add garlic, fresh ginger, cloves, lemon peel, celery leaf, or fennel bulb and tops instead of leek. Tie the ingredients in a bundle using cheesecloth and kitchen string. Leave it in the pot throughout the cooking process, and discard when finished making stock or poaching. See specific recipes for specific bouquet garni blends.

Techniques

How to get the most flavor and visual appeal out of your ingredients—and create healthy, low-fat recipes at the same time

CHIFFONADE CUT

In an unorthodox twist, this technique for cutting leafy vegetables and herbs into ribbonlike strips can be used for chicken breasts. It works especially well for many recipes, like stir-fries, that call for quick-cooking strips of breast meat. Chiffonade-cut herbs and leafy vegetables can be used in sautés or sauces, as garnish, or raw as a bed for many different types of salads. Chiffonade-cut ingredients contribute to an attractive presentation of any dish.

How to: Roll several leaves of lettuce, spinach, herbs, arugula, radicchio, chicory, or cabbage (or chicken breast) in a tight bundle, leaf around leaf around leaf. Holding the tight bundle of leaves together, slice to the required thickness, usually ⅛ to ¼ inch. The result is a pile of curled, ribbonlike strips.

DEGLAZE

This technique is a step in the sauté process. The bits of browned food and juices adhering to the sauté pan are remoistened and cooked with a flavorful liquid. The result is an instant pan sauce to drizzle or spoon over the chicken breasts that were cooked in the pan and set aside to keep warm.

How to: First pour off any excess fat from the pan. Over medium-high heat, add 1 cup of dry white or red wine, stock, poaching liquid, or juice to the pan, stirring and scraping to loosen the bits stuck to the bottom. Continue cooking over medium heat, stirring constantly until the liquid has almost completely reduced. Add spices, herbs, or other ingredients to the liquid, stir, heat through, and drizzle over the cooked chicken breasts. Serve immediately.

JULIENNE CUT OR MATCHSTICK

This technique for making very thin, matchstick-shaped strips of food—such as vegetables, *cooked* chicken breast, and citrus rind—is best for quick-cooking recipes and for garnishes.

How to: First cut the food into1½-inch lengths, pile them together and cut into very thin strips (about ⅛ inch) lengthwise. For chicken or other bulkier ingredients cut the strips individually and uniformly.

REDUCE

This technique thickens a sauce or strengthens the flavor of a liquid, such as juice or stock.

How to: Cook the ingredients over high heat to decrease the amount of liquid according to directions in the recipe.

COOKING TECHNIQUES, BASICS, AND TIPS

Poach (page 25)
Bake & Roast (page 51)
Sauté (page 73)
Stir-Fry (page 95)
Steam (page 106)
Grill, Broil & Smoke (page 119)
Stove Top (page 146)

Tools

This equipment goes hand in hand with cooking low-fat, more healthful, and flavorful chicken breasts

NONSTICK COOKWARE

Herein lies the key to more healthful low-fat dishes. There are many new nonstick surfaces from a variety of manufacturers. These much improved, high-quality, guaranteed-not-to-stick pots and pans no longer have chipping problems and don't require those silly-looking little nylon utensils. Coating a nonstick surface lightly with vegetable oil cooking spray is a simple way to further reduce the amount of butter and oil required in a recipe, and to prevent sticking. All the recipes in this book were tested with the newest pots, pans, and skillets from Farberware Millennium. This tough new nonstick surface was a veritable lifesaver, both in the cooking and cleaning-up stages. But most new nonstick surfaces are vast improvements over original nonstick surfaces like Teflon. Department store cooking demonstrations are a great way to experience Millennium and other nonstick cookware before you buy.

STEAMING POTS

Handmade Chinese steam baskets and stainless steel pans with separate steaming inserts are just two of a variety of possibilities. Turn to the "Steam" section on page 106 for the complete picture.

WOKS

A carbon-steel-forged Chinese wok is only one way to go with stir-fry. Once it is seasoned (or broken in, so to speak) and well used, the surface gets slippery and the food slides off with very little oil needed. Woks with nonstick surfaces are okay for low-fat cooking in general; however, the high heat required for a quick-cooking stir-fry is usually too hot for many of these surfaces. Check instructions on your nonstick wok before placing it over a high flame.

GRILLS

The "Grill, Broil & Smoke" section on page 119 has lots of information on grilling and smoking. One new and very improved aid to low-fat *indoor* grilling is the countertop electric grill. It's another way to shave off fat calories, and the full flavor of marinades come alive just as they would in outdoor grilling. These new grills de-smoke as they cook. As with any electrical device, the heat is harder to control, so use at your own risk! The Bistro Grill, by Farberware, came in handy during the testing process, and the chicken breasts cooked on it looked grilled and tasted great.

PEPPER MILLS

Pepper is a very important ingredient in many types of cooking. Almost all the recipes in this book call for white or black pepper. Both should be freshly ground from a separate pepper mill, which is the only way to get that special punch from this spice. Keep your supply as fresh as possible for the best flavor.

Recipes for All Occasions

LISTED THE WAY WE USE THEM

So, you're planning a brunch for Sunday. Why not make it a buffet? Perhaps on the patio or under the trees. Selecting recipes that are easily prepared in advance and can be arranged on a buffet table without further attention to detail are the ones that will allow you to entertain in the most relaxed manner! Al Fresco and Picnic Fare lists quite a few recipes that are perfect for this or any outdoor dining situation. Shop through this recipe list not only with an occasion in mind, but with a taste on the tip of your tongue. For instance, when you want it "hot," the Southwestern, Asian, and other recipes with a hefty amount of chilies are all listed under, what else, Hot! Hot! Hot! With the recipes listed under Strictly Main Dish, you'll get your fill of dishes of substance, from hearty casseroles to everyday dishes both plain and fancy—for Tuesday night or Saturday eve.

These sections will help, inspire, and put this book to *work* for you.

CLASSICS

The Calorie-Conscious Versions

Tomato-Herb Sauce or Vinaigrette
Watercress Sauce
Chicken, Rice, and Spinach Filled Cabbage Rolls
Glazed Chicken Loaf
Crispy Oven-Fried Chicken Breasts
Chicken Cakes with Balsamic-Shallot Sauce
Chicken Breasts with Tomato and Basil Sauce on Linguine

Classic Rosemary Chicken Salad
Chicken with Fig and Port Wine Sauce
Crispy Chicken Cutlets on Garlic Mashed Potatoes
White Wine Coq au Vin
Chicken and Farm-Stand Vegetable Soup

PARTY FARE

Hot and Cold Buffets and Appetizers

Summer Rolls with Spicy Mint Dipping Sauce
Poached Chicken Breasts with Bean Ragout
Baked Chicken-Stuffed Zucchini
Balsamic Chicken Breasts with Vegetables en Papillote
Steamed Lemon Chicken Breast Bundles
Stuffed Chicken Rolls and Yellow Pepper Sauce
Chicken and Roasted Artichoke Risotto
Goat Cheese and Basil Stuffed Chicken Breasts
Crispy Ginger Chicken with Sake Dipping Sauce

AL FRESCO AND PICNIC FARE

For Baskets, Boxes, and Anything Under the Sun

Oregano Chicken with Herbed Tomatoes
Herbed Chicken Salad with Tomato Tabbouleh
Peanut and Sesame Chicken Salad
Grilled Rosemary Chicken, Asparagus, and Red Onion Salad
Smoked Chicken Salad with Horseradish Sauce and Apple Slaw
Dallas-style Barbecued Chicken
Caribe-style Chicken Breasts
Chicken and Snow Pea Rice Salad

STRICTLY MAIN DISH

Casual and Dressed Up

Poached Chicken Breasts Pesto
Chicken Pot Pie with a Potato Top
Herb and Mustard Baked Chicken with Fava Beans
Chicken with Mustard-Cream Sauce
Chicken Paillards with Mushrooms and Peppers
Chicken Breasts with Creamy Spring Onion Sauce
Sautéed Chicken Breasts with 20 Shallots
Lemon-Thyme Chicken Breasts
Champagne and Chanterelle Chicken Breasts
Orange Chicken and Peppers with Curly Noodles
Sweet and Sour Chicken Stir-Fry
Steamed Chicken Breast and Zucchini Bundles
Chicken Breasts with Roasted Onion Marmalade
Chicken in Red Wine Sauce with Pappardelle Pasta
Spinach Pasta with Chicken and Lentils
Tomato and Garlic Chicken with Wild Rice
Hearty Corn, Chicken, and Chile Soup

Chicken and Summer Vegetables with Pan-Fried Polenta
Honey-Mustard Chicken with Mushroom Ragout
Pan-Seared Chicken Breasts with Basil Sauce

HOT! HOT! HOT!

Southwestern, Asian, and Others with Chilies

Homemade Jalapeño Mayonnaise
Spicy Black Mushroom Sauce
Dijon and Fresh Horseradish Sauce
Shredded Ginger-Soy Chicken Salad
Spicy Szechwan Baked Chicken
Spicy Mexican Grilled Chicken Breasts with Sweet and Hot Citrus Vinaigrette
Southwestern Chicken Hash with Spicy Salsa
Spicy Chicken and 3-Bean Chili

SALADS

Warm to Cold, Vegetable to Fruit, Niçoise to à la Grecque

Basil Chicken and Pasta Salad
Lemony Artichoke, Parmesan, and Chicken Salad
Mediterranean Chicken and Green Bean Salad
Chicken and Fennel Salad with Thyme-Mustard Dressing
Roasted Chicken, Arugula, and Basil Salad
Chicken Niçoise Salad
Chicken with Basil, Endive, and Peppers
Chicken and Portobello Mushroom Salad
Smoked Chicken Breasts and Chopped Sweet Onion Salad

FINGER FOOD

And Other Handheld Delicacies

Pineapple and Chicken Salad with Peanuts
Shredded Chicken and Wild Rice Salad
Cheese and Mushroom Quesadillas with Salsa and Creamy Guacamole
Grilled Chicken Burgers with Tomato Chutney
Thai Chicken Satay with Peanut Dipping Sauce
Soft Tacos Filled with Grilled Chicken and Vegetables
Pot Stickers with Chinese Dipping Sauce

FAST FARE

Five-Minute Miracles

Mango Chutney Chicken
Chilled Chicken Breasts with Cucumber-Dill Sauce
Pizza with the Works!
Chicken Paillards with Walnuts and Parsley Sauce
Stir-Fried Chicken Breasts with Cabbage and Water Chestnuts
Chicken and Asparagus Stir-Fry
Soy and Lime Chicken Breasts Steamed in Sake
Fusilli with Chicken, Herbs, and Oven-Dried Tomatoes

Smoked Chicken Salad with Golden Caviar Sauce
Balsamic Chicken Skewers
Barley Risotto with Chicken and Vegetables
Escalopes of Chicken on Spinach with Lemon and Shallot Sauce
Chicken, Peas, and Pasta
Sautéed Chicken with Tarragon-Tomato Sauce

HERBS AND SPICES

Well-Seasoned Recipes

Blackened Cajun Chicken
Asian Orange-Glazed Chicken Breasts
Plum-Basted Chicken Breasts on Thyme Couscous
Chicken Braised in Apple Juice and Fresh Sage
8 Sauces to Serve with Hot or Cold Poached Chicken Breasts

VEGGIES AND FRUITS

Farm-Stand Influence

Chardonnay–Yellow Pepper Sauce
Apricot-Mustard Sauce
Pureed Fresh Vegetable Sauce
Asian Chicken, Potato, and Avocado Salad
Tarragon Chicken Breasts with Artichokes
Chicken with Grapefruit, Red Onion, and Radicchio
Glazed Chicken Breasts with Peach Chutney
Chicken-Vegetable Stir-Fry
Chicken and Melon Stir-Fry
Chicken Breasts with Fruit Salsa
Grilled Chicken with Papaya and Mango Relish
Smoked Chicken with Watercress Sauce over Pasta
Curried Chicken with Carrot and Onion
Cold Chicken Breasts with Pineapple Relish
Herbed Chicken Fricassee

ETHNIC

A World of Flavors

Vietnamese Shredded Chicken and Cabbage Salad
Tequila-Marinated Chicken Ceviche Salad
Paprika Chicken with Egg Noodles
Layered Chicken Enchiladas
Olive and Feta Stuffed Chicken Rolls
Sautéed Chicken Breasts with Fruity Coconut-Curry Sauce
Thai Chicken Breast Stir-Fry
Japanese Stir-Fry with Peas
Chicken Breasts with Chinese Black Bean Puree
Spicy Gazpacho with Chicken and Avocado
Caribbean Grilled Chicken
Creole-style Chicken Gumbo

Poach

For the naturally lean chicken breast, poaching is one of the most favorable of the low-fat cooking methods, and should never be confused with boiling. The poaching liquid slowly and gently simmers the skinless, boneless chicken breast to a tender and flavorful finish in just about 8 minutes. Never use just plain water. Poaching requires a flavored liquid, which can be made up of a variety of nonfat stocks, including chicken or vegetable, wines, and juices. Next comes the poaching bouquet. Fresh herbs and spices, aromatics, and acidic ingredients should be used abundantly to enhance this liquid since the chicken breasts will absorb all their flavors during cooking and while they cool to room temperature in the liquid in some cases (see page 26 for a list of creative poaching bouquets, or make one using the ingredients you have on hand). Once done, the delicate white poached breast meat lends itself to a wide variety of dishes, from ethnic flavored salads to appetizers fit for any party, or simply slice it and serve with a fruit- or herb-laced sauce drizzled on top or on the side. See pages 37–40 for a lineup of quick, fresh sauces to pair with poached chicken breasts. Instructions for the perfect poach can be found in the box on page 26.

A Recipe for the Perfect "Quick" Poach

Ingredients: 2 cups (or more) Defatted Chicken Stock, Herb and Wine Stock, Vegetable Stock, wine, or juice, plus 1 parsley sprig, 1 celery leaf, pinch of salt, and several peppercorns or a poaching bouquet containing the fresh herbs and spices of your choice (see Note). Four skinless, boneless chicken breast halves.

1. In a high-sided skillet, bring all the ingredients except the chicken to a simmer. Add the chicken breasts, arranging them in a single layer, and simmer for 8 to 10 minutes, or just until cooked throughout. The chicken will feel firm when pressed with the back of a fork. Let cool to room temperature in the liquid, if desired.

2. Shred or cut the cooked chicken into bite-size pieces, or slice on the diagonal, across the grain. Wrap tightly in plastic wrap if not using immediately, and then store in a plastic bag or airtight container for up to 2 days.

Note: Other ingredients may be added to the poaching liquid, such as 2 tablespoons lemon juice, 1 tablespoon lemon zest strips, 1 tablespoon dried herbs of your choice, whole cloves, or allspice berries.

Poaching Bouquets

Place the ingredients for a poaching bouquet together on a piece of cheesecloth, fold over two opposite ends to cover the ingredients, and tie the bag with the two free ends. The bouquet will impart flavors to the water or liquid and is easy to retrieve when the cooking is finished. Discard the bag after cooking the chicken breasts. A freshly assembled bouquet each time is a must. The following poaching bouquets will impart different types of ethnic flavors to cooking.

Asian: 1 piece fresh ginger, 2 star anise, green onions, garlic

Provençal: Garlic, chervil, tarragon, basil, chives, parsley

American: Parsley, garlic, onion, peppercorns, celery leaf, carrot

Mexican: Red bell peppers, cumin, cinnamon, parsley, lime zest

Southwestern: Red dried chile peppers, cilantro, citrus, ginger

Thai: Lemon grass, mint, coriander, lime, ginger, chilies

Caribbean: Chilies, allspice, curry, mint, cilantro, lime, ginger, coconut

Classical French Bouquet Garni: Bay leaf, fresh parsley sprigs, thyme, black peppercorns

OREGANO CHICKEN WITH HERBED TOMATOES

Serve with grilled crusty French or country-style bread. If you can't find yellow tomatoes, two red tomatoes will work just fine.

4 shallots, chopped
1 cup dry Champagne or other dry white wine
1 cup Defatted Chicken Stock (see page 18)
½ bunch fresh oregano leaves, or 2 teaspoons dried
Juice of 2 lemons
4 skinless, boneless chicken breast halves (about 1½ pounds)
Salt
1 large yellow tomato, sliced, then halved
1 large red tomato, sliced, then halved
1 teaspoon dried herbes de Provence
1 garlic clove, finely minced
1 tablespoon extra-virgin olive oil
Freshly ground white pepper
2 tablespoons chopped fresh parsley for garnish
Fresh oregano sprigs for garnish (optional)

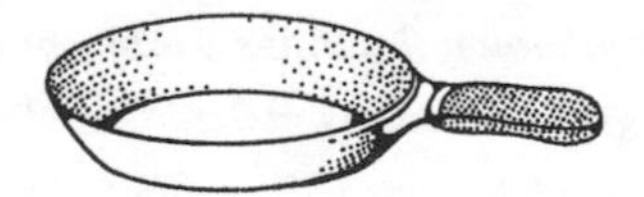

1. In a medium high-sided skillet, bring the shallots, Champagne or white wine, chicken stock, oregano, and lemon juice to a simmer. Add the chicken breasts, lightly salt the liquid, and poach until done, uncovered, about 8 to 10 minutes. Cool to room temperature in the poaching liquid.

2. Meanwhile, place the tomatoes in a shallow bowl. Sprinkle with the herbes de Provence, garlic, and oil, and season lightly with salt and pepper. Marinate for 20 minutes.

3. Slice the chicken. On 4 individual plates, arrange equal amounts of the marinated tomatoes. Place a sliced chicken breast in the center of each. Garnish with the chopped parsley and a sprig of oregano, if using.

Serves 4

Nutritional Breakdown: *313 calories, 6.2 g fat—18% calories from fat, 98.6 mg cholesterol, 1.2 g fiber, 318 mg sodium*

ASIAN CHICKEN, POTATO, AND AVOCADO SALAD

2 cups Defatted Chicken Stock (see page 18)
Poaching bouquet (see page 26), containing 2 pieces smashed lemon grass; 1-inch piece fresh ginger; quartered, ¼ teaspoon coriander seeds; and 5 black peppercorns
4 skinless, boneless chicken breast halves (about 1½ pounds)

Dressing

¼ cup fresh lime juice
2 tablespoons dry white wine
2 tablespoons chopped fresh cilantro
2 teaspoons honey
1 tablespoon reduced-sodium soy sauce or tamari
2 teaspoons fish sauce (available in Asian markets and some supermarkets)
2 tablespoons extra-virgin olive oil
3 tablespoons chopped green onion, green part only

1½ pounds new potatoes, boiled until tender, cooled, and quartered
2 tablespoons poaching liquid (reserved from poaching chicken)
Salt and freshly ground black pepper
1 small ripe avocado, peeled and sliced

1. In a medium high-sided skillet, bring the stock and bouquet to a boil, reduce to a simmer, and cook for 5 minutes. Add the chicken and poach uncovered, until done, about 8 to 10 minutes. Cool the chicken in the poaching liquid, wrap in plastic, and chill. Reserve the liquid.
2. To make the dressing, whisk the lime juice, white wine, cilantro, honey, soy sauce, and fish sauce together. Whisk in the oil in a thin stream until the ingredients are well combined. Stir in 2 tablespoons of the green onion.
3. In a bowl, toss the potatoes with the reserved liquid and remaining green onion. Season with salt and pepper.
4. Slice the chicken into thin rounds across the grain. Place in a bowl, drizzle on ½ cup of the dressing, and toss gently. Mound the potatoes in the center of a platter, and arrange the chicken and avocado slices around the edge. Top with a few grinds of pepper. Pass the remaining sauce in a bowl, if desired.

Serves 4

Nutritional Breakdown (includes 2 tablespoons of dressing per serving): *483 calories, 9.9 g fat—19% calories from fat, 100 mg cholesterol, 4.5 g fiber, 742 mg sodium*

MANGO CHUTNEY CHICKEN

There are many commercial chutneys available that can be substituted for the mango in this recipe. Try tomato or peach chutney. Each chutney has a distinct and explosive flavor and will partner well with poached or grilled chicken breasts. Serve this delicate fare with a side salad of assorted baby greens.

2½ cups Defatted Chicken Stock (see page 18)
4 skinless, boneless chicken breast halves (about 1½ pounds)
Salt
⅓ cup reduced-fat mayonnaise
3 tablespoons Major Grey's mango chutney, chopped
¼ teaspoon freshly ground white pepper
10 or more very thin slices reduced-calorie whole wheat bread, crusts removed, cut in triangles, and toasted just before serving
1 bunch baby parsley, trimmed into small sprigs, for garnish

1. In a medium high-sided skillet, bring the chicken stock to a simmer. Add the chicken breasts, lightly salt the liquid, and poach, uncovered, until done, about 8 to 10 minutes. Cool to room temperature in the poaching liquid. Remove the chicken to the bowl of a food processor fitted with the metal blade.

2. Process the chicken breasts to a smooth paste. Add the mayonnaise and mango chutney and process to mix well. Season the spread with salt and pepper to taste.

3. Spread the mango chicken on half of the toast triangles, place a parsley sprig on each, and cover with the remaining toast. Keep covered with plastic wrap until ready to serve.

Serves 4 to 8

Nutritional Breakdown: *405 calories, 8.4 g fat—18% calories from fat, 104 mg cholesterol, 7.4 g fiber, 1,049 mg sodium*

BASIL CHICKEN AND PASTA SALAD

2 cups Defatted Chicken Stock (see page 18)
1 cup dry white wine
6 black peppercorns
1 bay leaf
2 garlic cloves, smashed
4 skinless, boneless chicken breast halves (about 1½ pounds)
Salt
½ cup reduced-fat mayonnaise
½ cup plain nonfat yogurt
1 tablespoon white wine vinegar, preferably herb-flavored
1 garlic clove, finely minced
¼ cup poaching liquid (reserved from poaching chicken)
Freshly ground black pepper
½ pound fusilli, cooked al dente according to package instructions, cooled to room temperature
10 fresh basil leaves, stems removed, cut into chiffonade
1 head red leaf lettuce, leaves separated
1 large ripe tomato, peeled and diced, for garnish
Fresh basil leaves for garnish

1. In a medium high-sided skillet, bring the chicken stock, wine, peppercorns, bay leaf, and smashed garlic to a simmer and cook for 5 minutes. Add the chicken breasts, lightly salt the liquid, and poach, uncovered, until done, about 8 to 10 minutes. Cool to room temperature in the poaching liquid.

2. Strain the poaching liquid and reserve ¼ cup. Cut the chicken into bite-size pieces. Set aside.

3. In a small bowl, whisk together the mayonnaise, yogurt, vinegar, and minced garlic. Thin with the poaching liquid to the desired consistency. Season with salt and pepper to taste.

4. In a large mixing bowl, combine the chicken and pasta. Drizzle on the dressing and toss to coat well. Add the basil chiffonade and toss to mix well. Line a deep serving platter with the lettuce leaves. Mound on the chicken salad and garnish with tomato and basil leaves.

Serves 4

Nutritional Breakdown: *436 calories, 9.56 g fat—20% calories from fat, 107 mg cholesterol, 1.8 g fiber, 688 mg sodium*

VIETNAMESE SHREDDED CHICKEN AND CABBAGE SALAD

A visit to the Asian market can turn up all sorts of interesting and tasty tidbits to serve on the side of this salad: crunchy peas, tiny spicy rice crackers, even shrimp puffs that melt in your mouth.

2 cups Defatted Chicken Stock (see page 18)
4 skinless, boneless chicken breast halves (about 1½ pounds)
Salt
2–3 red serrano or jalapeño chilies, seeded and very finely minced
2 large garlic cloves, crushed
2 tablespoons sugar
½ cup Vietnamese or other fish sauce (available in Asian markets and some supermarkets)
¼ cup fresh grapefruit juice
¼ cup fresh lime juice
3 large carrots, peeled and grated
1 pound red cabbage, finely shredded
1 pound napa cabbage, finely chopped
¼ cup finely chopped fresh mint
½ cup chopped fresh cilantro leaves
¼ cup toasted sesame seeds
Grapefruit sections, peeled, pith and membrane removed, for garnish
Fresh cilantro and mint sprigs for garnish

1. In a medium high-sided skillet, bring the chicken stock to a simmer. Add the chicken breasts, lightly salt the liquid and poach, uncovered, until done, about 8 to 10 minutes. Cool to room temperature in the poaching liquid.
2. Shred the breast meat and chill, covered, with plastic wrap.
3. In the bowl of a mini food processor, place the chilies, garlic, and sugar. Process to a spreadable consistency. Transfer to a small bowl, stir in the Vietnamese fish sauce, grapefruit juice, and lime juice. Stir to mix well.
4. In a large mixing bowl, combine the carrots, cabbages, chicken, mint, cilantro, and sesame seeds and toss to mix. Drizzle on the dressing and toss to coat the ingredients. Marinate for 5 minutes.
5. Serve on 4 individual plates or a serving platter. Garnish with grapefruit sections and cilantro and mint sprigs.

Serves 4

Nutritional Breakdown: *362 calories, 4 g fat—10% calories from fat, 119 mg cholesterol, 7 g fiber, 854 mg sodium*

PINEAPPLE AND CHICKEN SALAD WITH PEANUTS

Wrap this salad in lettuce leaves instead of pitas for a super low-calorie presentation.

2 cups Defatted Chicken Stock (see page 18)
1 cup fresh pineapple juice
4 skinless, boneless chicken breast halves (about 1½ pounds)
Salt
1 cup pineapple chunks
1 celery stalk, thinly sliced
3 green onions, thinly sliced
¼ cup chopped, unsalted, roasted peanuts
3 tablespoons Major Grey's chutney, chopped
2 tablespoons fresh lemon juice
1 teaspoon grated lemon zest
½ teaspoon medium curry powder, or more to taste
¼ cup reduced-fat mayonnaise
½ cup nonfat sour cream
2 tablespoons poaching liquid (reserved from poaching chicken)
1 tablespoon finely chopped parsley
Freshly ground white pepper
4 whole wheat pitas

1. In a medium high-sided skillet, bring the chicken stock and pineapple juice to a simmer. Add the chicken breasts, lightly salt the liquid, and poach, uncovered, until done, about 8 to 10 minutes. Cool to room temperature in the poaching liquid. Reserve 2 tablespoons of the poaching liquid.

2. Coarsely chop the chicken and place in a large mixing bowl with the pineapple chunks, celery, green onions, and peanuts. Toss to combine.

3. In a small bowl, combine the chutney, lemon juice, lemon zest, curry powder, mayonnaise, sour cream, poaching liquid, and parsley. Stir to mix well.

4. Drizzle the dressing over the chicken mixture and toss gently to coat. Season with salt and pepper to taste. Cover tightly with plastic wrap and chill for at least 1 hour before serving. Serve in the pitas.

Serves 4

Nutritional Breakdown: *536 calories, 7.3 g fat—12% calories from fat, 102 mg cholesterol, 4.4 g fiber, 848 mg sodium*

SHREDDED CHICKEN AND WILD RICE SALAD

This salad wrapped up in soft leaves of Boston lettuce makes delicious finger food; calorie-conscious by nature, it is rather fun to eat.

6 cups Defatted Chicken Stock (see page 18)
1 garlic clove, peeled
Salt
4 ounces uncooked wild rice, soaked in hot tap water for 30 minutes and drained
Poaching bouquet (see page 26), containing 1½-inch piece peeled ginger, 4 peppercorns, 1 stalk celery with tops (halved), 1 garlic clove, parsley sprigs, fresh tarragon sprig
4 skinless, boneless chicken breast halves (about 1½ pounds)
3 tablespoons reduced-sodium soy sauce or tamari
3 tablespoons rice wine vinegar
1 tablespoon dark sesame oil
1 tablespoon light canola or other vegetable oil
1 red bell pepper, seeded and finely chopped
2 cups (about 2 bunches) loosely packed arugula leaves, cut into chiffonade
3 large green onions, white and green parts, thinly sliced
¼ cup toasted sesame seeds
2 heads Boston lettuce, leaves separated, chilled

1. In a heavy medium saucepan, bring 4 cups of the chicken stock and the garlic to a boil. Lightly salt the liquid. Add the wild rice, cover, reduce the heat to very low, and cook until tender, about 45 minutes. Remove from the heat and let stand 15 minutes, covered. Drain thoroughly and remove the garlic clove. Fluff the rice and place it in a large mixing bowl to cool.
2. In a medium high-sided skillet, bring the remaining 2 cups of chicken stock and the poaching bouquet to a simmer. Add the chicken breasts and poach, uncovered, until done, about 8 to 10 minutes. Cool at room temperature in the poaching liquid.
3. Shred the breasts into very thin strips, then cut the strips in half. Chill, covered.
4. In a glass jar with a tight-fitting lid, combine the soy sauce, vinegar, and oils. Shake vigorously to combine.
5. In a large mixing bowl, combine the chicken breast, wild rice, bell pepper, arugula, green onions, and half the toasted sesame seeds. Toss to mix.
6. Drizzle on the dressing. Toss to mix

well. Arrange the lettuce leaves as cups on a platter. Fill the lettuce cups to about one-third full and sprinkle on the remaining sesame seeds. Serve while the lettuce is still cold, folding over the leaves to form "packets" as they are eaten.

Serves 6 to 8 as a generous appetizer or first course

Nutritional Breakdown: *292 calories, 8.9 g fat—28% calories from fat, 65.7 mg cholesterol, 1.7 g fiber, 1,278 mg sodium*

SUMMER ROLLS WITH SPICY MINT DIPPING SAUCE

These make great summer appetizers. The rice paper wrappers are fun to work with, but a bit fragile, so be prepared for a few sheets to tear as you get the hang of handling it.

2 cups Defatted Chicken Stock (see page 18)
4 skinless, boneless chicken breast halves (about 1½ pounds)
Salt
1½–2 cups fresh sprouts, such as bean, sunflower, and onion, cut into 1-inch pieces
3 large green onions, white and green parts, chopped
2 tablespoons minced fresh mint leaves
1 tablespoon fish sauce (available in Asian markets and some supermarkets)
1 tablespoon fresh lime or lemon juice
18–24 8-inch rice paper wrappers (available in Asian markets and some supermarkets)
20–24 long strips of green onion, green part only, blanched for 15 seconds in boiling water and dried on a paper towel

Mint Sauce

⅓ cup very strong mint tea (boil mint leaves in water for 5 minutes and steep for 15)
¼ cup rice wine vinegar
1 teaspoon Chinese hot chile paste (available in Asian markets and some supermarkets)
2 garlic cloves, finely minced
1 tablespoon sugar
2 tablespoons reduced-sodium soy sauce or tamari

1. In a medium high-sided skillet, bring the chicken stock to a simmer. Add the chicken breasts, lightly salt the liquid, and poach, uncovered, until done, about 8 to 10 minutes. Cool to room temperature in the poaching liquid.

2. Shred the breasts into very thin strips, then chop with a cleaver.

3. In a medium bowl, combine the chopped chicken, sprouts, chopped green onions, mint, fish sauce, and lime juice. Toss to mix well.

4. To make the mint sauce, in a jar with a tight-fitting lid, place the mint tea, vinegar, chile paste, garlic, sugar, and soy sauce. Shake to mix well. Place in a small bowl.

5. In a shallow bowl filled with very hot water, dip two or three rice paper wrappers at a time. When soft and pliable, after about 30 seconds, remove the wrappers to a work surface covered with a clean cotton dishcloth and pat off the excess water with a paper towel. Place a rounded tablespoonful of the filling in the center of each wrapper. Fold in the left and right sides, fold the bottom flap up, and cover with the top flap. The bundle should form a rectangular log shape. Tie each roll in the center with a green onion strip. Place the rolls on a serving platter and cover with a moistened dish towel so that the rice paper does not dry out. Pass the mint dipping sauce on the side.

Serves 4 to 6

Nutritional Breakdown: *419 calories, 3.1 g fat—7% calories from fat, 111 mg cholesterol, 1.9 g fiber, 778 mg sodium*

An Array of Puree

What can you add to stocks to create low-fat and nonfat sauces so rich in flavor that butter-laden sauces will never be missed again? This list of ingredients is long and wonderful, including pureed carrot, artichoke, spinach, watercress, tomato, beet, and white corn (strained after pureeing). Even aromatics such as oven-roasted or smoked onions, garlic, leeks, and shallots can be incorporated. The vegetables should be well peeled, cut, and precooked before transferring to a blender. Add wine or Vegetable Stock (see recipe on page 17) in equal amounts and blend to a smooth puree. For a silky finish, add a teaspoon of olive oil, and season with a pinch of salt and freshly ground white pepper to taste. Heat and reduce slightly if necessary for a thicker sauce. Flavored stock sauces tend to be thinner than flour-thickened sauces or butter sauces. The real difference is the intensity and purity of flavor, and the lack of fat or butter is a great bonus. These sauces are at their best when paired with low-fat chicken breasts.

CHILLED CHICKEN BREASTS WITH CUCUMBER-DILL SAUCE

The cucumber-dill sauce should be served the same day it's made or it will get watery.

2 large cucumbers, peeled, seeded, halved, and very thinly sliced
1 teaspoon kosher salt
2 cups Defatted Chicken Stock (see page 18)
¼ cup fresh lemon juice
Poaching bouquet (see page 26), containing 1 stalk celery with leaf, ½ leek sliced lengthwise, parsley sprigs, 6 black peppercorns, 1 large piece lemon zest, and ½ bay leaf
4 skinless, boneless chicken breast halves (about 1½ pounds)
Salt
2 tablespoons white wine vinegar
2 tablespoons finely chopped fresh dill
1 cup low-fat or nonfat sour cream
Freshly ground white pepper
Fresh dill sprigs for garnish

1. Place the cucumber slices around the inside of a colander, sprinkle on the salt, and drain for 30 minutes. Rinse, pat dry, and chop very fine.
2. In a medium high-sided skillet, bring the chicken stock, lemon juice, and poaching bouquet to a simmer. Add the chicken breasts, lightly salt the liquid, and poach, uncovered, until done, about 8 to 10 minutes. Cool at room temperature in the poaching liquid. Chill, covered in plastic wrap.
3. In a medium bowl, combine the vinegar, dill, chopped cucumber, and sour cream and stir to mix. Season with salt and pepper to taste. Cover with plastic wrap and refrigerate.
4. Slice the chicken and arrange on 4 individual plates. Spoon the cucumber sauce beside the chicken and garnish with dill sprigs.

Serves 4

Nutritional Breakdown: *283 calories, 3.3 g fat—11% calories from fat, 99.7 mg cholesterol, 2.0 g fiber, 1,095 mg sodium*

8 SAUCES TO SERVE WITH HOT OR COLD POACHED CHICKEN BREASTS

All of these sauces can be made in advance. They are especially delicious as chicken salad dressings, as dipping sauces, on sandwiches, and, as the title above indicates, when served on hot and cold poached chicken breasts. This is, to say the least, a versatile group of recipes you will endlessly enjoy.

DIJON AND FRESH HORSERADISH SAUCE

½ cup nonfat sour cream
½ cup plain nonfat yogurt
3 tablespoons freshly grated horseradish
2 tablespoons coarse-grain mustard
Salt
1 tablespoon clover blossom honey

1. In a medium bowl, whisk the sour cream, yogurt, horseradish, mustard, salt, and honey together until well combined.
2. Serve at room temperature or refrigerate, covered, until well chilled.

Makes 1½ cups

Nutritional Breakdown (includes 2 tablespoons of sauce per serving): *310 calories, 3.6 g fat—11% calories from fat, 99.2 mg cholesterol, 2.5 g fiber, 1,200 mg sodium*

PUREED FRESH VEGETABLE SAUCE

¼ cup water
¾ cup dry white wine, (such as Chardonnay or Sauvignon Blanc)
⅓ cup peeled, chopped carrot
⅓ cup sliced celery
⅓ cup chopped zucchini
½ cup chopped onion
½ cup peeled and seeded chopped tomato
Salt and freshly ground white pepper

1. In a medium saucepan, bring the water, wine, carrot, celery, zucchini, and onion to a boil. Cover and simmer over low heat for 10 minutes.
2. Transfer to a blender, add the tomato, and blend until smooth. Season with salt and pepper to taste.
3. Return the sauce to the pan and bring to a boil until reduced by half. Serve warm or at room temperature.

Makes about 1 cup

Nutritional Breakdown (includes ¼ cup of sauce per serving): *235 calories, 2.2 g fat—9% calories from fat, 98.6 mg cholesterol, 1.2 g fiber, 260 mg sodium*

CHARDONNAY–YELLOW PEPPER SAUCE

1 large yellow bell pepper, cored, seeded, and coarsely chopped
¾ cup dry Chardonnay
¾ cup Defatted Chicken Stock (see page 18)
3 garlic cloves, chopped
Salt and freshly ground white pepper
½ cup low-fat or nonfat sour cream (optional for cold sauce)

1. In a medium saucepan, combine the yellow pepper, wine, chicken stock, and garlic. Simmer over medium heat until the peppers are soft, about 10 minutes. Remove the peppers with a slotted spoon, set aside, and continue simmering until the stock is reduced by one half the original amount. Set aside to cool.
2. In a blender or the bowl of a food processor fitted with the metal blade, combine the stock and peppers and process until smooth. Season with salt and pepper to taste. Serve hot or cover and chill. Stir in the sour cream just before serving, if desired.

Makes 1 cup, or 1½ cups with the sour cream

Nutritional Breakdown (includes ¼ cup of sauce per serving): *320 calories, 3.6 g fat—10% calories from fat, 99.2 mg cholesterol, 3.1 g fiber, 1,220 mg sodium*

APRICOT-MUSTARD SAUCE

1 cup apricot preserves
2 teaspoons white wine vinegar
2 tablespoons Dijon mustard
Pinch of white pepper
Pinch of salt

1. In a small saucepan, heat the preserves, vinegar, mustard, pepper, and salt over low heat until warmed through.
2. Transfer to a blender and blend until smooth. Transfer to a serving bowl and serve warm or at room temperature.

Makes about 1 cup

Nutritional Breakdown (includes 2 tablespoons of sauce per serving): *449 calories, 3.7 g fat—7% calories from fat, 98.6 mg cholesterol, 3.17 g fiber, 1,178 mg sodium*

SPICY BLACK MUSHROOM SAUCE

12 dried black Oriental or oyster mushrooms, softened in 1 cup of hot water, drained and liquid reserved
2 teaspoons peanut oil
½ cup bottled chili sauce
¼ cup medium-dry sherry
2 tablespoons reduced-sodium soy sauce or tamari
2 tablespoons red wine vinegar
2 tablespoons dark brown sugar
2 teaspoons Szechwan chile paste with garlic (available in Asian markets and some supermarkets)

1. Wash the mushrooms well, pat dry, and chop fine.
2. In a small skillet, heat the peanut oil. Cook the mushrooms over low heat until tender and the moisture has evaporated, about 5 minutes. Set aside.
3. In a small saucepan, combine the chili sauce, sherry, soy sauce, vinegar, brown sugar, chile paste, and ⅓ cup of the reserved mushroom liquid and bring to a boil. Cook until thick, about 7 or 8 minutes. Stir in an additional ⅓ cup mushroom liquid. Serve warm or at room temperature.

Makes about 1 cup

Nutritional Breakdown (includes 2 tablespoons of sauce per serving): *373 calories, 6.1 g. fat—15% calories from fat, 98.7 mg cholesterol, 3.9 g fiber, 1,521 mg sodium*

WATERCRESS SAUCE

Salt
4 bunches fresh watercress, well washed, leaves removed, and stems discarded
2 tablespoons low-fat or nonfat sour cream
1 tablespoon fresh lemon juice
Freshly ground black pepper

1. In a large pot of boiling, lightly salted water, cook the watercress leaves for 3 minutes. Drain, reserving ½ cup of the liquid.
2. Transfer the watercress to a blender and, adding 1 tablespoon of the reserved cooking liquid at a time, blend to a puree. Transfer to a bowl, cover, and chill.
3. Just before serving, stir in the sour cream until well combined, and then stir in the lemon juice. Adjust the seasoning with salt and pepper to taste.

Makes about 1 cup

Nutritional Breakdown (includes ¼ cup of sauce per serving): *258 calories, 3.2 g fat—11% calories from fat, 98.6 mg cholesterol, 2.6 g fiber, 1,067 mg sodium*

A Salad Suggestion: Toast Those Sesame Seeds

Toasted sesame seeds make a glorious 2-minute garnish for a chicken salad. Toasting is essential to bringing out that uniquely nutty and somewhat smoky flavor found deep within the sesame seed. It also changes the color of the seeds from white to a toasty brown, and creates a tiny crunch that bursts with flavor. ***How to:*** To toast, set a small, dry nonstick sauté pan over moderate heat. Add the sesame seeds and stir constantly until light to medium brown in color, 2 to 4 minutes. Such little things, such big flavor!

TOMATO-HERB SAUCE OR VINAIGRETTE

Tomato Sauce

1 tablespoon olive oil
½ cup chopped onion
2 garlic cloves, finely minced
½ teaspoon sugar
1 teaspoon dried basil
1 teaspoon dried oregano
1 teaspoon freshly ground black pepper
1 teaspoon salt
1 can (28 ounces) plum tomatoes, drained and chopped

Vinaigrette

1 tablespoon red wine vinegar
1 teaspoon chopped fresh basil
1 tablespoon extra-virgin olive oil
Salt and freshly ground black pepper

1. In a small saucepan, heat the oil. Add the onion and garlic and cook over medium heat until tender but not brown, about 3 minutes.
2. Stir in the sugar, basil, oregano, pepper, salt, and tomatoes. Cook over medium heat, partially covered, for 8 to 10 minutes. Serve hot, or continue with the recipe to make a vinaigrette.
3. For vinaigrette, cool the tomato sauce to room temperature. In a jar with a tight-fitting lid, combine the sauce with the red wine vinegar, chopped basil, and oil. Shake to combine well. Season with salt and pepper to taste. Shake again just before serving.

Makes about 2 cups

Nutritional Breakdown (includes ¼ cup of tomato-herb sauce or 2 tablespoons vinaigrette per serving): *358 calories, 8.4 g fat—21% calories from fat, 98.6 mg cholesterol, 5 g fiber, 1,908 mg sodium*

HOMEMADE JALAPEÑO MAYONNAISE

2 jalapeño chilies, roasted, peeled, deveined, seeded, and finely minced
1 tablespoon fresh lime juice
1 tablespoon fresh lemon juice
⅔ cup low-fat mayonnaise
1 tablespoon finely chopped fresh cilantro (optional)

1. In a bowl, mix together the jalapeños, lime and lemon juices, and mayonnaise.
2. Cover and chill. Fold in the cilantro just before serving, if desired.

Makes about ¾ cup

Nutritional Breakdown (includes 2 teaspoons mayonnaise per serving): *255 calories, 4.7 g fat—17% calories from fat, 98.6 mg cholesterol, 0.1 g fiber, 542 mg sodium*

POACHED CHICKEN BREASTS PESTO

Serve over angel hair pasta, or atop grilled French or Italian bread slices.

1 cup dry white wine
1 cup Defatted Chicken Stock (see page 18)
Juice of 1 lemon
Poaching bouquet (see page 26), containing ½ juiced lemon (cut in pieces), 4 whole black peppercorns, and 1 bunch flat-leaf parsley
4 skinless, boneless chicken breast halves (about 1½ pounds)
Salt
1 cup flat-leaf parsley leaves
1 cup fresh basil leaves
3 garlic cloves
1 tablespoon toasted pine nuts
1¾ tablespoons extra-virgin olive oil
1 cup poaching liquid (reserved from poaching)
Freshly ground white pepper
1½ tablespoons finely grated Parmesan cheese

1. In a medium high-sided skillet, bring the wine, chicken stock, ½ of the lemon juice, and the poaching bouquet to a simmer and cook for 5 minutes, covered. Add the chicken breasts, lightly salt the liquid, and poach, uncovered, until done, about 8 to 10 minutes. Remove the chicken and cover to keep warm. Drain, reserving 1 cup of the liquid.

2. In a blender or mini food processor, blend or process the parsley, basil, remaining lemon juice, garlic, and pine nuts. With the motor running, add the olive oil in a thin stream until a soft paste forms.

3. Strain the reserved poaching liquid and return to the skillet. Stir in the pesto and bring to a simmer over medium heat. Return the chicken breasts to the pan to heat through, about 2 minutes.

4. Transfer the breasts to a platter with a slotted spoon, and cover to keep warm. Increase the heat to high and continue cooking to reduce the liquid until a sauce forms, about 2 to 3 minutes. Season with salt and pepper to taste and spoon over the chicken. Sprinkle on the Parmesan and serve hot.

Serves 4

Nutritional Breakdown: *331 calories, 11 g fat—30% calories from fat, 100 mg cholesterol, 0.7 g fiber, 357 mg sodium*

TEQUILA-MARINATED CHICKEN CEVICHE SALAD

These flavors are reminiscent of the ones used in the marinated seafood salads served in Mexico and Spain.

1 cucumber, cut lengthwise, seeds scraped out with a spoon, and thinly sliced
½ cup fresh lime or lemon juice
1 cup fresh orange juice
2–3 tablespoons best-quality light tequila
½ small red onion, halved and thinly sliced
½ small yellow onion, halved and thinly sliced
2 small garlic cloves, finely minced
3 tablespoons finely minced fresh cilantro
½ teaspoon Tabasco sauce, or 1 teaspoon seeded, finely minced jalapeño
1 teaspoon finely chopped orange zest
1 teaspoon finely chopped lime or lemon zest
¼ teaspoon salt
1 green bell pepper, seeded, ½ finely diced and ½ cut into very thin matchsticks
1 red bell pepper, seeded, ½ finely diced and ½ cut into very thin matchsticks
4 cups ¾-inch diced pieces poached chicken breast (see poaching instructions on page 26)
Large lettuce leaves, chilled
12 red and yellow cherry tomatoes, halved

1. Drain the sliced cucumber in a strainer for 30 minutes.
2. In a large glass or pottery bowl, combine the lime or lemon juice, orange juice, tequila, red and yellow onions, garlic, cilantro, Tabasco or jalapeño, orange and lime or lemon zests, salt, cucumbers, diced bell peppers, and chicken pieces and mix well. Cover tightly with plastic wrap and marinate, refrigerated, for 2 to 4 hours.
3. Drain the salad in a fine mesh strainer and discard the marinade. On 4 to 6 individual serving plates, arrange several lettuce leaves to make a bed. Mound the salad on lettuce and garnish with the bell pepper matchsticks and tomatoes.

Serves 4 to 6

Nutritional Breakdown: *333 calories, 6.2 g fat—18% calories from fat, 108 mg cholesterol, 2.9 g fiber, 238 mg sodium*

GINGER-SOY SHREDDED CHICKEN SALAD

This salad is great served with a finely grated cabbage and carrot slaw.

2 cups Defatted Chicken Stock (see page 18)
2 1-inch slices fresh ginger, peeled
3 tablespoons sherry vinegar
2 green onions, green part only
3 black peppercorns
½ teaspoon salt
4 skinless, boneless chicken breast halves (about 1½ pounds)

Dressing

3 tablespoons chopped peeled fresh ginger
1 tablespoon rice wine vinegar
4 tablespoons red wine vinegar
1 tablespoon honey
1 teaspoon sugar
1 tablespoon sodium-reduced soy sauce or tamari
1 tablespoon chopped fresh basil leaves
2 tablespoons chopped green onion, white part only
⅛ teaspoon crushed red pepper, or more to taste
1–2 tablespoons water
2 tablespoons peanut oil
1½ tablespoons toasted sesame seeds
2 tablespoons chopped green onion, green part only
Salt (optional)

1. In a medium high-sided skillet, bring the chicken stock, ginger, vinegar, green onions, peppercorns, and salt to a simmer and cook for 5 minutes, covered. Add the chicken breasts and poach, uncovered, until done, about 8 to 10 minutes. Cool to room temperature in the poaching liquid. Drain and pat dry.

2. To make the dressing, in a blender or food processor, combine the ginger, vinegars, honey, sugar, soy sauce, basil, the white part of the green onion, red pepper, and water and process until pureed. With the motor running, add the oil slowly and process until smooth.

3. Shred the chicken and place in a bowl. Add the sesame seeds, green part of the green onion, and dressing. Mix well. Season with salt, if desired. Chill.

Serves 4

Nutritional Breakdown: *309 calories, 9.7 g fat—29% calories from fat, 98.6 mg cholesterol, 0.9 g fiber, 971 mg sodium*

LEMONY ARTICHOKE, PARMESAN, AND CHICKEN SALAD

The shredded, raw artichoke in a salad is a wonderful change from salad greens. It has a more hearty texture, with a delicate and interesting taste.

4 small artichokes
⅓ cup plus 1 tablespoon fresh lemon juice
2 tablespoons balsamic vinegar
1 tablespoon chopped fresh oregano, or 1 teaspoon dried
15 tablespoons extra-virgin olive oil
4 cups shredded poached chicken breast (see poaching instructions on page 26)
Salt and freshly ground black pepper
2 cups mixed baby lettuce, torn if necessary
2 cups coarsely chopped arugula leaves
¼ cup shaved Parmesan cheese
¼ cup chiffonade-cut fresh basil
Large shavings (2 tablespoons) Parmesan cheese for garnish

1. Working quickly so the artichokes do not discolor, snap off any tough outer leaves from each artichoke, trim the ends, cut through the center lengthwise, and remove the purple inner leaves and hairy choke with a spoon.
2. With a very sharp stainless steel knife, a mandoline, or the sharp blade side of a stainless steel grater, shred or shave the artichokes very thinly. Place all the shaved artichokes in a large nonreactive mixing bowl with the ⅓ cup lemon juice and immediately toss to coat with the juice to keep the artichokes from discoloring. Marinate for 5 minutes in the juice.
3. In a glass jar with a tight-fitting lid, combine the tablespoon of lemon juice, vinegar, oregano, and oil. Shake well.
4. Place the shredded chicken in a small bowl. Drizzle on the balsamic dressing and toss to coat well. Adjust the seasoning with salt and pepper.
5. Add the lettuce, arugula, ¼ cup shaved Parmesan cheese, and basil to the artichokes and gently toss to mix well.
6. Divide the artichoke salad among salad bowls. Mound the shredded chicken breast in the center. Top with the large shreds of Parmesan. Pass the pepper mill.

Serves 4

Nutritional Breakdown: *355 calories, 12 g fat—30% calories from fat, 110 mg cholesterol, 7.7 g fiber, 288 mg sodium*

MEDITERRANEAN CHICKEN AND GREEN BEAN SALAD

1¼ cups Defatted Chicken Stock (see page 18)
¾ cup dry red wine
2 black peppercorns
2 whole garlic cloves
4 fresh basil leaves
Salt
4 skinless, boneless chicken breast halves (about 1½ pounds)
⅔ cup reduced poaching liquid
1 pound green beans, trimmed
¾ cup nonfat plain yogurt
2 tablespoons fresh lemon juice
1 teaspoon dried oregano
2 teaspoons dried basil
½ teaspoon dried thyme
Freshly ground black pepper
2 small red onions, halved and thinly sliced
2 tablespoons chopped toasted almonds
2 tablespoons coarsely chopped French, Italian, or Greek oil-cured olives
12 cherry tomatoes, halved

1. In a medium high-sided skillet, bring the chicken stock, wine, peppercorns, garlic, basil leaves, and a pinch of salt to a simmer over medium heat. Add the chicken breasts, and poach, uncovered, until done, about 8 to 10 minutes. Let cool to room temperature in the poaching liquid.

2. Transfer the chicken with a slotted spoon to a platter. Cover with plastic wrap and chill. Strain the remaining poaching liquid into a small saucepan and reduce by two thirds over high heat, about 10 to 15 minutes. Set aside.

3. Steam the green beans just to crisp-tender, about 4 minutes. Immediately plunge into a bowl of ice water or run under cold water to stop the cooking process. Do not overcook. Cover and chill.

4. In a jar with a tight-fitting lid, combine the yogurt, lemon juice, oregano, dried basil, thyme, reduced poaching liquid, and a pinch of salt and pepper and shake to mix well.

5. In a large mixing bowl, combine the beans, onions, almonds, and olives. Drizzle on three-quarters of the dressing and toss gently to mix well. Adjust the seasoning with salt and pepper to taste. Marinate for 10 to 15 minutes.

6. Slice the chicken breasts thinly on the diagonal across the grain into ¼-inch slices. Arrange on 4 individual serving plates. Mound the bean salad beside the slices and garnish with the tomatoes. Drizzle the remaining dressing on the chicken slices, and top with a turn of the pepper mill.

Serves 4

Nutritional Breakdown: *364 calories, 6.7 g fat—17% calories from fat, 99.4 mg cholesterol, 6.1 g fiber, 528 mg sodium*

HERBED CHICKEN SALAD WITH TOMATO TABBOULEH

Tabbouleh Salad

½ cup bulgur
1¼ cups boiling spring water
2 tablespoons peeled, seeded, and finely diced plum tomato
1 tablespoon minced green onion
1 tablespoon minced flat-leaf parsley
1 tablespoon minced fresh mint
1 tablespoon minced fresh basil
2 tablespoons extra-virgin olive oil
Salt and freshly ground black pepper

Chicken Breast and Herb Marinade

¼ cup low-fat or nonfat yogurt
2 ripe plum tomatoes, peeled, seeded, and finely diced
2 tablespoons finely chopped green onion, white part only
1 tablespoon minced flat-leaf parsley
1 teaspoon minced fresh basil
½ teaspoon grated lemon zest
4 cups (about 1½ pounds) shredded poached chicken breast (see poaching instructions on page 26)
Salt and freshly ground black pepper

Roasted Green Onions

8 large green onions
1 teaspoon extra-virgin olive oil
Salt and freshly ground black pepper
12 cherry tomatoes for garnish

1. To make the tabbouleh, heat a medium nonstick skillet over high heat, add the bulgur, and toast, shaking the pan and stirring constantly until lightly browned, about 4 to 5 minutes. Transfer to a medium bowl and add the boiling water. Cover tightly with plastic wrap and let stand, about 30 minutes. When tender, but still a bit chewy, transfer to a strainer and press to remove any excess water. Return to the bowl and add the tomato, green onion, parsley, mint, basil, and oil and toss to combine. Season with salt and pepper to taste. Cover tightly with plastic wrap and marinate for 1 hour at room temperature.

2. Meanwhile, to make the chicken, in a large bowl, combine the yogurt, tomatoes, green onion, parsley, basil, lemon zest, and shredded chicken breast. Season with salt and pepper, and toss genty to mix. Cover tightly with plastic wrap and marinate, refrigerated, for 1 hour.

3. To make the roasted green onions, preheat the oven to 450°F. Brush the onions with the oil. Place on a baking sheet and roast for 8 to 10 minutes, or until browned and tender. Wipe off the excess oil with paper towels. Season with salt and pepper to taste. Set aside.

4. To assemble the salad, toss the tabbouleh to fluff up the bulgur. Toss the marinated chicken breast to mix well. On a large serving platter, make a bed of tabbouleh. Pile the chicken in the center. Garnish with the roasted green onions and cherry tomatoes.

Serves 4 to 6

Nutritional Breakdown: *446 calories, 15.4 g fat—31% calories from fat, 131 mg cholesterol, 5.6 g fiber, 143 mg sodium*

No-Fail, No-Fat Poaching Liquid

Although some poaching liquids in this chapter may call for additional ingredients, you can safely follow this recipe for a perfect poaching liquid.

Standard Poaching Liquid

1 cup dry white wine and 1 cup Defatted Chicken Stock (see page 18) or 2 cups Defatted Chicken Stock
2 to 3 shallots, or 1 onion, peeled and quartered
½ carrot, peeled and thinly sliced
1 celery leaf, chopped
1 leek, white part only, cleaned and coarsely chopped
4 to 6 black peppercorns
Pinch of salt

In a poacher, stockpot, or high-sided skillet, combine all the ingredients and bring to a simmer. Proceed as directed in the individual recipes in this chapter.

POACHED CHICKEN BREASTS WITH BEAN RAGOUT

This was influenced by a dish created at Pinto Bistro in Los Angeles by Octavio Becerra, the outstanding executive chef. This is probably the most complicated recipe in this book, but certainly one of the most rewarding. For information about the French-style Herb and Wine Stock, see pages 16–17.

Herb and Wine Stock

1½ teaspoons canola or other vegetable oil
1 large yellow onion, chopped
1 large leek, washed and chopped
½ stalk celery, chopped
1 whole head garlic, loose outside papery skin removed, cut in half crosswise
1 large fennel bulb, diced
½ bunch fresh thyme
3 bay leaves
½ bunch flat-leaf parsley
1 bottle (750 ml) dry white wine, preferably Chardonnay
2 cups spring water

Chicken Breasts and Bean Ragout

16 garlic cloves, unpeeled
3 teaspoons extra-virgin olive oil
1 tablespoon canola or other vegetable oil
¾ pound mixed fresh mushrooms (such as chanterelle, porcini, shiitake, portobello, and oyster), diced
1 cup dry white wine
4 cups Herb and Wine Stock
1 cup uncooked beans (such as chestnut, cranberry, or great northern), soaked overnight, undrained
2 sprigs fresh thyme
2 bay leaves
½ onion, quartered
½ medium carrot, peeled and halved
4 sage leaves
4 skinless, boneless chicken breast halves (about 1½ pounds)
Salt and freshly ground white pepper
1 tablespoon finely chopped fresh chives

1. To make the Herb and Wine Stock, in a large saucepan, heat the oil. Add the onion, leek, celery, garlic, and fennel and cook over medium heat until the vegetables are translucent, but not browned, about 4 minutes. Add the thyme, bay leaves, parsley, wine, and water. Bring to a boil. Reduce the heat and simmer for 1 hour. Pour through a fine mesh strainer. Chill, covered.

2. To prepare the garlic preheat the oven to 300°F. In a small baking dish, add the garlic and 2 teaspoons of the olive oil and stir to coat well. Cover tightly with foil and bake for 45 minutes, or until the garlic is soft. Squeeze the pulp of 12 cloves into a small bowl. Peel the remaining 4 and reserve for garnish.
3. In a large sauté pan, heat the canola oil. Add the mushrooms and cook over medium high heat until the mushroom liquid evaporates, about 8 minutes. Add ½ cup of the wine and cook until the liquid is almost evaporated. Add 1 cup of the stock, bring to a boil, reduce the heat, and simmer until the mushrooms are tender, about 7 minutes. Set aside.
4. In a medium saucepan, combine the soaked beans with ¾ cup of their soaking water, 1 cup of the stock, thyme, bay leaves, onion, carrot, and sage. Bring to a boil, reduce the heat, and simmer until the beans are tender, about 45 minutes. Strain the beans, reserving the liquid. Combine the beans and mushrooms and set aside.
5. In a medium high-sided skillet, bring the bean liquid, 1 cup of the stock, and the remaining ½ cup wine to a simmer. Add the chicken breasts and gently poach, uncovered, until done, about 8 to 10 minutes. Remove from the liquid with a slotted spoon and keep warm.
6. To make the sauce, warm the remaining 1 cup stock and pour into a blender. Add the roasted garlic puree and the remaining 1 teaspoon olive oil and blend until smooth. Season with salt and pepper to taste. Return to the pan.
7. To assemble the dish, heat the beans and mushrooms. Heat the sauce. Place equal amounts of bean and mushroom ragout in the bottoms of 4 shallow bowls. Place the chicken breasts on top of the beans, and spoon on the sauce. Garnish with the roasted garlic cloves and chives.

Serves 4

Nutritional Breakdown: *710 calories, 7.1 g fat—9% calories from fat, 98.6 mg cholesterol, 16.8 g fiber, 185 mg sodium*

What To Do with Leftover Poaching Liquid?

Use it again for another poach or as a sauce base. This flavorful liquid is not a stock in itself, but can be enhanced with additional vegetables and herbs for another use. Strain the poaching liquid through cheesecloth before refrigerating for up to 2 days, or freezing (see instructions for freezing stock on page 18). If reusing the broth for another poach or for a stock, add more strongly flavored ingredients, if necessary.

CHICKEN AND FENNEL SALAD WITH THYME-MUSTARD DRESSING

These poached chicken breasts are permeated with smoky tones from the ham, and freshened with the anise fennel.

3 cups plus 1 tablespoon defatted, low-sodium chicken stock
4 ounces smoked ham, diced
4 skinless, boneless chicken breast halves (about 1½ pounds)
1 tablespoon Dijon mustard
1 tablespoon coarse-grain mustard
½ teaspoon minced garlic
2 tablespoons minced onion
¼ cup low-fat or nonfat yogurt
¼ cup nonfat sour cream
2 teaspoons extra-virgin olive oil
3 teaspoons chopped fresh thyme leaves
Salt and freshly ground black pepper
2 medium fennel bulbs, trimmed, quartered, cored, and thinly sliced
2 tablespoons fresh lemon juice

1. In a medium high-sided skillet, bring 3 cups of the chicken stock and the ham to a simmer over medium heat and cook for 10 minutes. Add the chicken breasts to the liquid and poach, uncovered, until done, about 8 to 10 minutes. Cool to room temperature in the poaching liquid. Discard the ham.

2. In a blender or the bowl of a food processor fitted with the metal blade, process the mustards, garlic, onion, yogurt, sour cream, oil, 1 tablespoon chicken stock and 2 teaspoons of the thyme until smooth.

3. Cut the chicken into bite-size chunks and transfer to a large mixing bowl. Drizzle on the dressing and gently toss to mix well. Season with salt and pepper to taste.

4. In another large bowl, toss together the fennel, lemon juice, and a scant amount of salt and pepper. Divide the fennel evenly among 4 large plates. Mound the chicken chunks on top and sprinkle on the remaining thyme. Pass the pepper mill.

Serves 4

Nutritional Breakdown: *344 calories, 7.5 g fat—20% calories from fat, 114 mg cholesterol, 5.1 g fiber, 1,213 mg sodium*

Bake & Roast

Baking and roasting are high atop the list of low-fat cooking methods. Many of the recipes in this section can even be prepared ahead of time and then popped in the oven just before the dish is served. These recipes tend to take a little longer on the preparation end of the process than stir-fries or sautés, but the baking or roasting time is usually within 30 minutes since chicken breasts cook relatively quickly, and little attention is required during the baking time. The variety of different baking and roasting recipes is extraordinary. Just think of bubbling, homey, one-dish casseroles filled with lots of flavorful ingredients. Think of all the time saved. Think of all the calories saved—all with no loss of flavor. Some of the recipes in this chapter are ideal for special occasions and for entertaining. Olive and Feta Stuffed Chicken Rolls on page 71 are fancy enough to be served on your best china. Chicken Pot Pie (page 54) with bubbling tender chicken breast pieces, spring vegetables, and a potato top is definitely "homey gourmet" . . . if there is such a thing. Even the everyday favorites found in this chapter, like Glazed Chicken Loaf (page 61); Chicken, Rice, and Spinach Filled Cabbage Rolls (page 56); Pizza with the Works! (page 60); and tantalizing Layered Chicken Enchiladas (page 68) are excellent, and all low in fat and calories. Just set the oven for 350°F. (or as directed) and dig into these wonderful recipes.

Chicken Breasts in a Paper Pouch or, as the French Say, *en Papillote*

In searching out methods and techniques of cooking chicken breasts that are intrinsically low fat but also fun, I found one that is becoming more popular in this country. Properly called *en papillote,* this French technique is cooking food in a parchment paper pouch. (Aluminum foil may be substituted, but it isn't as romantic, so the French would definitely give this suggestion the thumbs-down.) The delicate, lean, skinless, boneless chicken breast meat cooks in its own juices and joins with the other ingredients *en papillote,* bubbling together in the no-leak pouch. The pouch puffs up or inflates during cooking, which is a distinct trademark of this method of baking chicken breasts. When each *papillote* is delivered to the diner and slit through the top to reveal the cooked food within, the unique presentation is enhanced by a burst of enticing aromas. When the ends are tied with kitchen string, the package makes its own attractive serving dish. Remember to fill the pouch with quick-cooking ingredients, like matchstick-cut vegetables and chopped herbs, so that everything is perfectly done at the same time. (See pages 67 and 72 for recipes.)

ROASTED CHICKEN, ARUGULA, AND BASIL SALAD

Take the ingredients commonly used in pesto sauce, create a salad dressing with bursting flavors and the crunch of toasted pine nuts on top, and serve it with crispy croutons made from a French or Italian loaf. You can use grilled chicken for this recipe as well as baked.

4 boneless chicken breast halves (about 1½ pounds), skin on for roasting only
Salt and freshly ground black pepper
1 cup chiffonade-cut fresh basil leaves
3 tablespoons red wine vinegar
1 tablespoon extra-virgin olive oil
2 bunches arugula, stemmed and cut into chiffonade
1 tablespoon finely grated Parmesan cheese
1 tablespoon toasted pine nuts for garnish

1. Preheat the oven to 375° F. Season the chicken breasts under the skin with salt, pepper, and ¼ cup of the basil. Place in a baking dish coated with nonstick spray and roast for 30 to 35 minutes, or until the juices run clear and the chicken is cooked through.

2. When cool enough to handle, remove the skin and discard. Cut the chicken into bite-size pieces and set aside.

3. In a jar with a tight-fitting lid, place the vinegar and oil. Shake well.

4. In a large mixing bowl, combine the arugula, the remaining ¾ cup basil, and the chicken pieces. Drizzle on the dressing and toss to mix. Season with salt and pepper. Sprinkle on the grated Parmesan and toss again.

5. Divide the chicken salad among 4 serving plates. Garnish with toasted pine nuts.

Serves 4

Nutritional Breakdown: *255 calories, 7.9 g fat—29% calories from fat, 99.8 mg cholesterol, 1.5 g fiber, 173 mg sodium*

CHICKEN POT PIE WITH A POTATO TOP

This wonderful-looking dish is great for a special family dinner.

2 pounds baking potatoes, peeled and cubed
2 cups nonfat milk
Salt and freshly ground white pepper
½ cup low-fat buttermilk
1 tablespoon finely grated Parmesan cheese
4 skinless, boneless chicken breast halves (about 1½ pounds), cut into bite-size pieces
3 teaspoons canola or vegetable oil
4 shallots, very thinly sliced
1 garlic clove, minced
1 small leek, white part only, washed, quartered lengthwise, and thinly sliced
2½ cups Defatted Chicken Stock (see page 18)
½ pound mushrooms, stemmed and sliced
⅓ cup dry white wine
2 medium carrots, peeled and cut into matchsticks
1 cup peas
2 tablespoons cornstarch, dissolved in 3 tablespoons water
1½ tablespoons finely chopped flat-leaf parsley
1 teaspoon finely chopped fresh thyme
1 tablespoon finely chopped fresh chives for garnish

1. In a large saucepan, combine the potato cubes, milk, and 2 cups water, or more, to cover. Bring to a boil over medium-high heat, lightly salt, and cook until the potatoes are tender, about 12 to 15 minutes. Drain and mash with the buttermilk in a mixing bowl until no lumps remain. Season with salt and pepper. Add ½ tablespoon of the grated Parmesan. Stir to mix well and set aside.

2. Season the chicken with salt and pepper. In a large nonstick skillet, heat 1 teaspoon of the oil. Add the chicken and cook over medium-high heat just until browned, about 3 minutes. Remove to a platter and set aside.

3. In the same skillet, heat 1 more teaspoon of the oil. Add the shallots, garlic, and leek and sauté, stirring frequently over medium heat, until tender. Add 1¼ cups of the chicken stock, bring to a boil, and cook for 3 minutes to reduce slightly. Transfer to a bowl. Set aside.

4. In the same skillet, heat the remaining 1 teaspoon of oil. Add the mushrooms and cook over medium heat until the mushroom liquid has evaporated, about 5 minutes. Add the remaining

1¼ cups stock, wine, carrots, and peas and bring to a simmer. Cook until the vegetables are crisp-tender, about 4 minutes. Remove the vegetables with a slotted spoon and set aside. Increase the heat and reduce the stock by one third, about 8 minutes.

5. Lower the heat, stir in the cornstarch mixture, and simmer until the sauce is thick, about 3 to 4 minutes more. Remove from the heat and set aside.

6. Add the chicken, parsley, and thyme to the pan, and season with salt and pepper to taste.

7. Preheat the oven to 450° F. Lightly coat a 1½-quart high-sided ovenproof baking dish (such as a soufflé dish) with cooking spray. Fill with the chicken, all the vegetables, and the sauce.

8. Top with the mashed potatoes and smooth to cover the surface of the chicken mixture completely. Set the dish on a larger baking sheet and bake for 20 to 25 minutes, or until the chicken is done. Turn the heat to broil. Sprinkle the potato top with the remaining ½ tablespoon Parmesan and brown under the broiler for about 20 to 30 seconds. Watch carefully! Sprinkle the top with the chopped chives. Serve hot.

Serves 4

Nutritional Breakdown: *657 calories, 8.8 calories from fat, 105 mg cholesterol, 7. 1,161 mg sodium*

Grape Leaves, Fig Leaves, and Chicken Breasts

These two types of leaves add both good looks and great taste to your chicken breasts. Their flavor is subtle, but it comes right through. When you wrap a chicken breast in either of these leaves, tie it shut, and cook it (either on the grill or in the oven), the essence from the grape or fig leaf imparts a distinctive flavor. Begin by washing the leaves well. Lightly spray one side with vegetable oil cooking spray. Place the chicken breast, salt and pepper to taste, and a few of your favorite fresh herbs in the center of the leaf and fold in the edges to make a package. Place them opening side down on an ovenproof baking sheet lightly sprayed with vegetable oil cooking spray, and bake at 350° F. for 15 to 20 minutes, or until done throughout. Serve in the leaves and let each person remove the chicken breast from its natural package. You begin to sense Napa, Provence, or Tuscany in the chicken breast. And, naturally, a leaf doesn't add a drop of fat to the feast.

CHICKEN, RICE, AND SPINACH FILLED CABBAGE ROLLS

This updated version of a classic dish is surprisingly hearty.

12 large green cabbage leaves
2 teaspoons extra-virgin olive oil
2 skinless, boneless chicken breast halves (about ¾ pound), finely chopped
¼ medium onion, finely chopped
½ medium carrot, peeled and finely chopped
¼ teaspoon dried rosemary
¼ teaspoon salt
½ teaspoon freshly ground black pepper
1 pound fresh spinach leaves, stemmed
1½ cups cooked brown rice
1 large egg, beaten
2 tablespoons finely grated Parmesan cheese
Pinch of nutmeg
½–1 cup Defatted Chicken Stock (see page 18)
Freshly cracked black pepper

1. Fill a large bowl with ice-cold water. Bring a stockpot of lightly salted water to a boil. Blanch the cabbage leaves 4 at a time for about 1 minute, or until the thickest part bends easily. Plunge into the cold water. Drain on paper towels and pat dry.

2. In a heavy nonstick skillet, heat the oil. Add the chicken and cook in a single layer over medium heat for 3 minutes. Add the onion, carrot, rosemary, salt, and pepper, and cook until the vegetables are tender, about 5 minutes. Add the spinach, spreading it evenly over the other ingredients, cover, and cook until wilted, about 2 to 3 minutes more.

3. Transfer the chicken mixture to a large bowl to cool slightly. Add the cooked rice, egg, Parmesan, and nutmeg and stir to combine.

4. Preheat the oven to 350°F. Spray a 9 × 13-inch glass baking dish lightly with cooking spray.

5. Place the cabbage leaves, hard rib side up, on a flat work surface. Using a paring knife, trim off the thick portion down the center without cutting through to the other side. Turn the leaves over.

6. Divide the stuffing into 12 equal portions and place in the center of the leaves. Fold the trimmed end over the stuffing, fold in each side, and then roll up the top to form a bundle about 3 inches long.

7. Place the bundles, seam side down, in the baking dish. The bundles should be touching but not tightly packed together. Pour over the chicken stock. Bake for 20 to 25 minutes, or until the stuffing is cooked through. Sprinkle with freshly cracked pepper before serving.

Serves 4

Nutritional Breakdown: *294 calories, 7.1 g fat—21% calories from fat, 105 mg cholesterol, 6.9 g fiber, 523 mg sodium*

BAKED CHICKEN-STUFFED ZUCCHINI

Buy zucchini that are all the same size and length so that they cook evenly. Your choice of squash need not be limited to zucchini. Try round pattypan and crookneck yellow summer squash to make a trio of interesting stuffed shapes for this recipe. Serve it piping hot or warm on a buffet with equal success.

9 medium zucchini, trimmed
Salt
2 tablespoons extra-virgin olive oil
2 shallots, minced
1 pound mushrooms, stemmed and finely chopped
1 pound ground skinless, boneless chicken breast
1 cup fresh bread crumbs (see pages 12–13)
⅓ cup finely grated Parmesan cheese
¼ cup chopped flat-leaf parsley
Freshly ground black pepper

1. Finely chop 1 of the zucchini. Halve the remaining 8 zucchini lengthwise and scrape out the seeds.
2. Place the chopped zucchini in a small strainer. Sprinkle with a pinch of salt and let drain for 30 minutes. Sprinkle a scant amount of salt on the inside of each of the zucchini halves and place, cut side down, on paper towels to drain for 30 minutes. Pat both the chopped zucchini and the zucchini halves dry with paper towels.
3. Preheat the oven to 325° F.

4. In a large nonstick skillet, heat 1 tablespoon of the oil. Add the shallots and cook, stirring constantly over medium heat, until translucent, about 4 minutes. Add the mushrooms and a pinch of salt. Continue cooking until the mushroom liquid has evaporated and the mushrooms are brown, about 7 minutes. Transfer to a bowl and set aside.

5. Add the ground chicken breast to the skillet and cook, stirring constantly over medium-high heat, just until browned, about 4 minutes. Add to the mushrooms.

6. In a clean, large, nonstick skillet, heat the remaining 1 tablespoon of oil. Cook the chopped zucchini over medium heat until tender, about 3 minutes. Add to the chicken mixture, along with the bread crumbs, half of the Parmesan, and half of the parsley. Season with salt and pepper to taste.

7. Mound the mixture evenly into the scooped-out centers of the zucchini halves. Arrange them in a decorative ovenproof baking dish. Bake for 20 to 25 minutes, or until the zucchini is tender. In the last 5 minutes of baking, sprinkle the tops with the remaining Parmesan, parsley, and a few grinds of pepper. Serve hot or warm.

Serves 4 to 6

Nutritional Breakdown: *406 calories, 13 g fat—28% calories from fat, 72.2 mg cholesterol, 6.8 g fiber, 461 mg sodium*

HERB AND MUSTARD BAKED CHICKEN WITH FAVA BEANS

1 pound fava beans, removed from the pods
3 tablespoons coarse-grain Dijon mustard
2 tablespoons extra-virgin olive oil
2 shallots, minced
3 large garlic cloves, minced
1 tablespoon chopped fresh thyme
1 teaspoon very finely chopped fresh rosemary leaves
4 skinless, boneless chicken breast halves, cut into quarters (about 1½ pounds)

2 teaspoons unsalted butter
¼ cup red wine vinegar
¼ cup light red wine (such as Pinot Noir or Beaujolais)
2½ cups Defatted Chicken Stock (see page 18)
2 tablespoons tomato paste
Salt and freshly ground black pepper
Fresh thyme sprigs for garnish

1. Bring a pot of water to a boil, drop in the fava beans, and blanch for 3 minutes. Drain, cool, and peel off the skin.
2. In a small mixing bowl, combine 2 tablespoons of the mustard, 1 tablespoon of the oil, the shallots, garlic, thyme, and rosemary, and mix to a paste.
3. Place the chicken pieces in a baking dish and rub all sides evenly with the mixture. Cover tightly with plastic wrap and marinate for 1 hour.
4. Preheat the oven to 350° F. In a large nonstick skillet, heat the remaining 1 tablespoon of oil and 1 teaspoon of the butter. Add the chicken pieces and brown on all sides over medium-high heat, about 2 to 3 minutes. Transfer to a baking dish, cover tightly with foil, and bake for 20 to 25 minutes, or until the chicken pieces are tender and done throughout.
5. To the skillet, add the vinegar and boil until the liquid is almost evaporated. Deglaze the pan with the red wine and reduce by half, stirring constantly, over high heat, about 3 minutes. Add the chicken stock and tomato paste and continue cooking over high heat for 5 to 6 minutes more, or until the sauce is reduced by half. Pour into a clean saucepan.
6. In the skillet, heat the remaining 1 teaspoon butter. Add the beans and cook over medium heat for 2 to 3 minutes. Add to the sauce, bring to a simmer, stir in the remaining tablespoon of mustard, and cook until the beans are tender. Adjust the seasoning with salt and pepper to taste.
7. To assemble, use a large decorative platter. Remove the beans from the sauce with a slotted spoon and place on the platter. Nestle the chicken pieces over the beans and spoon over the sauce. Decorate the platter with sprigs of fresh thyme.

Serves 4 to 6

Nutritional Breakdown: *393 calories, 10.9 g fat—26% calories from fat, 104 mg cholesterol, 4.8 g fiber, 1,324 mg sodium*

PIZZA WITH THE WORKS!

½ pound ground skinless, boneless chicken breast
¾ cup chopped onion
¾ cup chopped bell pepper
1 cup thinly sliced mushrooms
2 small garlic cloves, minced
1 tablespoon cornmeal
2 9-inch premade frozen pizza doughs, whole wheat if possible, thawed
Tomato-Herb Sauce (see page 40)
1½ cups shredded low-fat or part-skim mozzarella
⅓ cup finely grated Romano cheese
Red pepper flakes

1. In a large nonstick skillet lightly sprayed with cooking spray, cook the chicken over medium-high heat for 2 to 3 minutes. Add the onion, bell pepper, mushrooms, and garlic and cook, stirring constantly until done, about 3 to 4 minutes. Pour into a fine mesh strainer and let drain over a bowl. Set aside.

2. Preheat the oven to 400°F.

3. Spray 2 9-inch round pizza pans (or baking sheets) with oil cooking spray. Sprinkle the cornmeal evenly onto the two pans. Place the pizza dough on the pans and push into the inner rim to secure. Spoon the sauce evenly over the pizza dough. Divide the chicken mixture over the sauce. Distribute the mozzarella on top and sprinkle with the Romano cheese and red pepper flakes.

4. Bake in the center of the oven for 10 to 12 minutes, or until the crust is browned and the edges are crisp. Serve with more red pepper flakes, if desired.

Serves 2 to 4

Nutritional Breakdown: *518 calories, 16.2 g fat—28% calories from fat, 57.6 mg cholesterol, 5.6 g fiber, 1,426 mg sodium*

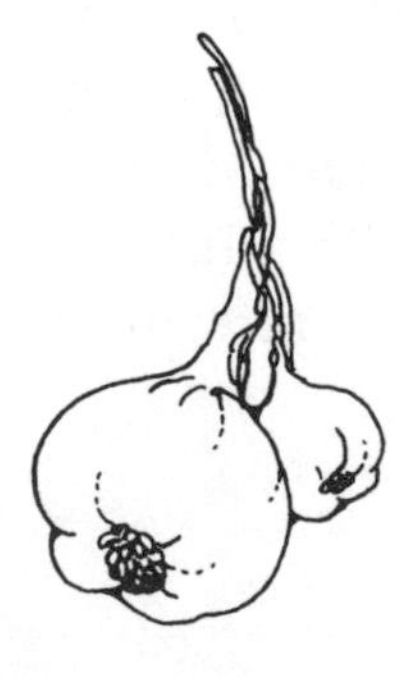

GLAZED CHICKEN LOAF

To make homemade bread crumbs, place 7 slices of home-style white bread in the bowl of a food processor fitted with the metal blade and process until crumbled. Place the crumbs on a baking sheet and dry in the oven at 250°F. for 15 minutes.

1 tablespoon canola or other vegetable oil
½ cup minced onion
½ cup minced green onion
2 teaspoons minced garlic
½ cup minced celery
½ cup minced red bell pepper
½ cup minced peeled carrot
2 pounds ground skinless, boneless chicken breast
5 large egg whites, beaten
¾ cup ketchup
1 cup unseasoned dried bread crumbs (homemade if possible)
½ teaspoon ground nutmeg
½ teaspoon ground cumin
½ teaspoon ground coriander
1 teaspoon freshly ground white pepper
1 teaspoon salt
3 tablespoons dark brown sugar

1. Preheat the oven to 350°F.
2. In a large nonstick skillet, heat the oil. Add the onion, green onion, garlic, celery, bell pepper, and carrot and cook over medium heat until softened, about 10 minutes. Set aside to cool.
3. In a large bowl, combine the ground chicken breast, egg whites, 4 tablespoons of the ketchup, and the bread crumbs. Mix well by hand.
4. In a small bowl, combine the nutmeg, cumin, coriander, and pepper. Stir into the cooled vegetable mixture. Combine with the chicken mixture until very well mixed.
5. In a small bowl, combine the remaining ½ cup ketchup and the brown sugar, and stir to mix well. Set aside.
6. Spoon the chicken mixture into 2 nonstick 9 × 5-inch loaf pans lightly sprayed with cooking spray. Spread the glaze on top to cover completely. Bake for 35 to 45 minutes, or until firm to the touch.
7. Let stand 10 minutes before removing the loaves to a cutting board. Slice thin and serve hot or cold.

Serves 6, or 4 with leftovers

Note: All the vegetables can be minced in a food processor fitted with the metal blade.

Nutritional Breakdown: *333 calories, 5.3 g fat—15% calories from fat, 87.6 mg cholesterol, 2 g fiber, 1,022 mg sodium*

PAPRIKA CHICKEN WITH EGG NOODLES

The combination of hot and sweet pepper makes this dish incredibly flavorful.

4 skinless, boneless chicken breast halves (about 1½ pounds)
2 tablespoons all-purpose flour
Salt and freshly ground black pepper
1 tablespoon extra-virgin olive oil
1 small onion, quartered, thinly sliced
3 large garlic cloves, crushed and minced
4–5 teaspoons sweet Hungarian paprika
½ teaspoon hot Hungarian paprika
1½ cups Defatted Chicken Stock (see page 18)
6–8 plum tomatoes, peeled and chopped (about 2 cups)
1½ tablespoons tomato paste
2 teaspoons unsalted butter, melted
2–3 tablespoons minced parsley
1 pound fresh egg noodles cooked al dente in lightly salted water, hot

1. Preheat the oven to 350° F. Dust the chicken with the flour and season with salt and pepper on all sides.
2. Coat a large skillet with cooking spray and heat the oil. Add the chicken and cook on high until brown, about 4 to 5 minutes, turning once halfway through. Transfer to an ovenproof baking dish.
3. To the same skillet, add the onion and garlic and cook over low heat until tender. Reduce the heat to low, sprinkle on the paprikas, stirring constantly, and cook for 2 minutes more. Pour in the chicken stock and tomatoes and stir in the tomato paste to mix well. Bring to a simmer and cook, uncovered, for 2 to 3 minutes to reduce slightly.
4. Pour the sauce over the chicken and bake for 7 to 9 minutes, or until the chicken is tender and done throughout.
5. Meanwhile, add the butter and 1 tablespoon of the parsley to the noodles and toss. Heat through in a sauté pan over medium-low heat. Serve the chicken breasts over the noodles, sprinkled with the remaining parsley. Drizzle a little more of the sauce over the chicken and pass the remaining sauce, if desired.

Serves 4 to 6

Nutritional Breakdown: *473 calories, 10.6 g fat—20% calories from fat, 141 mg cholesterol, 4.7 g fiber, 473 mg sodium*

SPICY SZECHWAN BAKED CHICKEN

This hot but satisfying dish has a complex flavor with just 1 tablespoon of oil.

1½ tablespoons Szechwan peppercorns, toasted
⅛ teaspoon dried crushed red pepper
1½ tablespoons coriander seed, toasted
½ teaspoon coarse salt
½ cup fresh cilantro leaves
¼ cup parsley leaves
2 teaspoons chopped orange or lemon zest
4 large garlic cloves, chopped
3 large shallots, chopped
2 teaspoons dark sesame oil
1 teaspoon vegetable oil
4 tablespoons reduced-sodium soy sauce or tamari
4 skinless, boneless chicken breast halves (about 1½ pounds)

1. Preheat the oven to 350°F.
2. In the bowl of a food processor fitted with the metal blade, combine the peppercorns, red pepper, coriander, and salt and process for 30 seconds. Scrape down the sides, add the cilantro, parsley, zest, garlic, shallots, and sesame oil and continue processing for 30 seconds more. Scrape into a small bowl.
3. In another small bowl, whisk together the vegetable oil and soy sauce. Dip the chicken breasts in the soy mixture. Place on a baking sheet lightly coated with cooking spray. Spread the herb mixture evenly on the chicken to cover completely. Marinate for 30 minutes.
4. Bake for 15 to 20 minutes, or until done throughout. Serve hot or warm.

Serves 4

Nutritional Breakdown: *249 calories, 5.9 g fat—22% calories from fat, 98.6 mg cholesterol, 1 g fiber, 1,192 mg sodium*

A Warning About Warming

Leaving the chicken breasts in the oven to keep them warm can be a disaster. When they're done, they're done. They will quickly reach the point of no return. To serve the chicken hot, remove the chicken breasts from the oven, cover them with a piece of aluminum foil, and try to serve them within 5 minutes.

CHEESE AND MUSHROOM QUESADILLAS WITH SALSA AND CREAMY GUACAMOLE

This creamy, rich dish will really satisfy your craving for a decadent treat, but still slides under the low-fat limit.

Guacamole

1 small avocado, peeled and cubed (about 1½ cups), pit reserved
½ cup nonfat sour cream
½ cup nonfat ricotta thinned with ½ tablespoon nonfat milk
3 tablespoons finely chopped red onion
2 tablespoons fresh lime juice
5 tablespoons finely chopped fresh cilantro leaves
½ teaspoon salt
½ teaspoon freshly ground black pepper

Salsa

4 ripe plum tomatoes, chopped
½ small red onion, chopped
1 small jalapeño chile, seeded, deveined, and minced
Pinch of salt

Quesadillas

2 teaspoons canola or corn oil
½ pound mushrooms, stemmed and sliced
Salt and freshly ground black pepper
2 skinless, boneless chicken breast halves (about ¾ pound), cut into ½-inch-wide strips
8 8-inch flour tortillas
1½ cups shredded reduced-fat Monterey Jack cheese
½ small red onion, very thinly sliced
¾ cup nonfat sour cream, at room temperature

1. To make the guacamole, in the bowl of a food processor, combine the avocado, sour cream, and ricotta and process until smooth. Transfer to a mixing bowl, stir in the red onion, 1 tablespoon of the lime juice, 2 tablespoons of the cilantro, the salt, and the pepper. Place the pit in the center, drizzle the remaining 1 tablespoon lime juice over the guacamole, and cover tightly with plastic wrap. Chill until ready to serve.

2. To make the salsa, in a small bowl, combine the tomatoes, onion, and jalapeño, and season with salt to taste. Set aside.

3. To make the quesadillas, preheat the oven to 375°F.

4. In a heavy nonstick skillet, lightly coated with cooking spray, heat 1 teaspoon of the oil. Add the mushrooms and cook over medium-high heat, stirring occasionally, until the mushrooms are lightly browned and the moisture has evaporated, about 7 minutes. Season with salt and pepper to taste. Set aside.

5. Wipe the skillet clean. Lightly coat with cooking spray and heat the remaining 1 teaspoon of oil. Add the chicken breast strips and cook over medium-high heat, stirring until done, about 4 to 5 minutes. Adjust the seasoning with a pinch of salt.

6. Lightly coat a baking sheet with cooking spray. Place 2 or more tortillas on the baking sheet. Sprinkle each tortilla with equal amounts of the cheese, chicken breast strips, mushrooms, onion, and the remaining chopped cilantro from the guacamole. Top each with another tortilla. Pinch the edges together. Bake for 5 minutes, or until the cheese is melted.

7. Remove the pit from the guacamole and stir. Place the quesadillas on a wooden cutting board and cut into quarters. Serve hot with the salsa, 2 teaspoons of the guacamole, and 1 tablespoon of the sour cream on the side. Pass the remaining sauces, if desired.

Serves 4 to 6 as an appetizer

Nutritional Breakdown (includes 2 teaspoons of guacamole per serving): *375 calories, 11.3 g fat—27% calories from fat, 44.6 mg cholesterol, 3 g fiber, 634 mg sodium*

Free-Range for Fancy Fare

Free-range chickens are the top of the line, so to speak. I buy them at Mrs. Gooch's, a wonderful gourmet organics and health food emporium that will soon be a coast-to-coast chain. I find the flavor of free-range birds to be a definite cut above that of commercially raised chickens. The taste and texture are remarkably different, and, in fact, free-range chickens are leaner than those that just sit around eating and getting fat. Free-range chicken breasts tend to be larger and more plump, a plus for making elegant meals for guests. And they roast beautifully. Yes, as you might guess, the price is a bit higher. In this case it's worth it, just like fresh herbs, good wine, and French or Italian extra-virgin olive oil are worth their higher price tags.

CHICKEN WITH MUSTARD-CREAM SAUCE

This sauce should be served warm. Heat it slowly in a small saucepan over low heat just long enough to warm throughout. Do not allow it to come to a simmer. Serve the chicken breasts hot with the sauce on the side.

4 skinless, boneless chicken breast halves (about 1½ pounds)
1 tablespoon unsalted butter, melted
4 tablespoons light brown sugar
¼ cup reduced-sodium soy sauce or tamari
2 tablespoons fresh lemon juice
3 tablespoons dry white wine
½ teaspoon freshly ground white pepper
Salt
1 cup low-fat sour cream
½ cup plain nonfat yogurt
1 teaspoon Worcestershire sauce
½ cup coarse-grain Dijon mustard
2 teaspoons dried basil
1 tablespoon finely chopped fresh basil

1. Line a baking pan with enough foil hanging over the sides to fold over the chicken to form a closed package. Place the in the foil, just touching.
2. In a small bowl, combine the melted butter, 3 tablespoons of the brown sugar, the soy sauce, lemon juice, wine, ¼ teaspoon of the pepper, and a pinch of salt. Brush the mixture onto the chicken and marinate, refrigerated, for 1 hour.
3. Meanwhile, in a saucepan, combine the remaining 1 tablespoon brown sugar, sour cream, yogurt, Worcestershire sauce, mustard, the remaining ¼ teaspoon pepper, and the dried basil and stir to mix well. Adjust the seasoning with salt. Set aside.
4. Preheat the oven to 375° F.
5. Fold the foil into a tight package over the chicken breasts and bake for 10 minutes. Open the foil, baste with the pan juices, and continue baking until done, about 5 to 7 minutes. Heat the sauce gently over low heat just before serving.
6. Slice the breasts and arrange on 4 plates. Stir the fresh basil into the sauce and put about 2 tablespoons of the sauce next to each piece of chicken. Pass the remaining sauce, if desired.

Serves 4 to 6

Nutritional Breakdown (includes 2 tablespoons of sauce per serving): *345 calories, 6.5 g fat—17% calories from fat, 107 mg cholesterol, 1 g fiber, 1,393 mg sodium*

BALSAMIC CHICKEN BREASTS WITH VEGETABLES EN PAPILLOTE

Substitute aluminum foil only if parchment paper is not available. Parchment makes a wonderful presentation, as it puffs up during cooking.

4 skinless, boneless chicken breast halves (about 1½ pounds)
3 tablespoons balsamic vinegar
Salt and freshly ground black pepper
3 tablespoons dry white wine or Defatted Chicken Stock (see page 18)
2 garlic cloves, minced
1 tablespoon chopped fresh basil, or 1½ teaspoons dried
2 teaspoons chopped fresh thyme, or 1 teaspoon dried
1 tablespoon chopped flat-leaf parsley
2 shallots, sliced
2 tablespoons extra-virgin olive oil
2 medium carrots, peeled and cut into 2-inch matchsticks
1 medium leek, white and light green parts, washed and cut into 2-inch matchsticks
½ red bell pepper and ½ yellow bell pepper, seeded and cut into 2-inch matchsticks

1. Place the chicken in a shallow glass baking dish and pour on the balsamic vinegar, salt, and pepper. Cover with plastic wrap and marinate for 15 to 20 minutes.
2. In a jar with a tight-fitting lid, combine the wine or stock, garlic, basil, thyme, parsley, shallots, and oil. Shake to mix well.
3. In a mixing bowl, combine the carrots, leek, and bell peppers and pour on the herb and oil mixture. Toss to coat the vegetables and marinate for 10 minutes.
4. Preheat the oven to 375°F.
5. Cut four 15 × 15-inch squares of parchment paper. Fold in half and crease to mark the center. Place the paper on a flat work surface.
6. In the center of one of the halves, place one quarter of the vegetables in a flat layer, reserving the remaining herb and oil mixture. Remove a chicken breast from the marinade and place on top of the vegetables. Stir the herb and oil mixture into the vinegar marinade and drizzle a bit over the chicken. Top with a grind of pepper. To close the parchment pouch, make an envelope by drawing the top flap of the paper over

the filling and folding in the edges together all around. Seal the packet with several more narrow folds around the edges to completely close. The package should seal tightly with the paper still loose over the filling to allow for expansion during cooking. Repeat to make 4 packets.

7. Place the packets on a baking sheet lightly coated with cooking spray. Bake for 25 to 30 minutes, or until the chicken is done and the parchment is puffed. Serve the packages in 4 shallow bowls and cut open at the table.

Serves 4

Nutritional Breakdown: *309 calories, 9.1 g fat—28% calories from fat, 98.6 mg cholesterol, 2.6 g fiber, 133 mg sodium*

LAYERED CHICKEN ENCHILADAS

2 teaspoons vegetable oil
1½ pounds ground skinless, boneless chicken breast
1 teaspoon finely minced garlic
Salt and freshly ground black pepper
½ cup chopped onion
2 tablespoons all-purpose flour
¾ cup Defatted Chicken Stock (see page 18)
¼ cup nonfat milk
1 can (4 ounces) chopped green chilies
1 teaspoon ground cumin
4 8-inch low-fat corn tortillas
1 can (10 ounces) fat-free enchilada sauce
3 cups chopped tomatoes
¾ cup grated reduced-fat sharp Cheddar cheese or crumbled reduced-fat Mexican cheese
½ cup chopped fresh cilantro leaves
½ cup picante sauce
6 tablespoons nonfat sour cream

1. Preheat the oven to 350° F.

2. In a heavy, medium nonstick skillet lightly coated with cooking spray, heat 1 teaspoon of the oil. Add the ground chicken and garlic, and cook until brown and crumbly, about 5 minutes. Remove from the pan. Drain in a strainer.

3. In the pan, heat the remaining 1 teaspoon oil. Add the onion and cook, stirring frequently, about 5 minutes. Set aside.

4. Sprinkle the flour into the pan. Whisk in the stock and milk in a thin, steady stream, and continue whisking until well mixed. Bring to a boil, reduce to a simmer, and continue cooking until the sauce is thick, about 3 minutes. Remove from the heat and add the chicken and onion to the sauce. Stir in the chilies and cumin. Stir to mix well.

5. Coat the bottom and sides of an 8-inch springform pan or round baking pan with cooking spray. Place one of the tortillas on the bottom. Spread on one quarter of the enchilada sauce and layer on one third of the tomatoes and one third of the chicken mixture. Top each layer with one quarter of the grated Cheddar cheese and some chopped cilantro. Repeat with two more layers and cover with the remaining tortilla. Spread enchilada sauce over the top tortilla, cover with foil, place on a baking sheet, and bake for 20 to 25 minutes.

6. Sprinkle on the remaining cheese and return to the oven just until melted and bubbling on top, about 5 minutes.

7. Let the layered enchilada sit for 10 minutes before cutting into 6 wedges. Top with chopped cilantro, 1½ tablespoons of picante sauce, and 1 tablespoon sour cream.

Serves 6

Nutritional Breakdown: *343 calories, 8.9 g fat—24% calories from fat, 82.9 mg cholesterol, 3.6 g fiber, 1,335 mg sodium*

Rules of the Roast

Say you're really tight on time. You don't even have time to read this, but you want to cook some chicken breasts and don't want to have to keep an eye on them. Check out the quick and easy marinades on page 129 and drop the chicken breasts in one for a few minutes. Or just squeeze on some lemon juice and chop up a few different kinds of fresh herbs and throw them on along with salt and freshly ground pepper to taste. Preheat the oven to 350°F. Lightly coat a nonstick ovenproof skillet (no plastic handles, please) with vegetable oil cooking spray, heat over medium-high heat, and add a teaspoon of olive oil or unsalted butter. Sear the breasts, about 2 minutes per side. Place the skillet in the oven. Then, go and do something and come back in 8 to 10 minutes, and eat! Easy? Always!

CRISPY OVEN-FRIED CHICKEN BREASTS

This recipe can also be used to make bite-size chicken breast fingers using the "fillets" that make perfect appetizers with cocktails or at a picnic. Do a Mediterranean version using Parmesan cheese instead of sesame seeds, oregano for the thyme, and eliminating the butter.

1½ cups cereal flakes (such as cornflakes or Special K, with no sugar), coarsely crushed into crumbs
⅓ cup sesame seeds, toasted and ground
1 teaspoon dried thyme, crumbled
2 teaspoons finely grated lemon zest, chopped
½ teaspoon salt
½ teaspoon freshly ground black pepper
2 medium egg whites
1 tablespoon fresh lemon juice
4 skinless, boneless chicken breast halves (about 1½ pounds)
1 tablespoon unsalted butter, melted and warm

1. Preheat the oven to 450° F. Lightly coat a metal baking sheet with cooking spray.

2. In a large plastic bag, combine the cereal crumbs, sesame seeds, thyme, lemon zest, salt, and pepper. Shake to mix, pour onto a plate, and spread out in a thin, even layer.

3. In a large shallow dish, whisk the egg whites and lemon juice until frothy. Coat the chicken breasts on all sides, letting the excess drip back into the dish.

4. Roll the chicken breasts in the crumbs, firmly pressing them into the surface.

5. Place the breasts on the baking sheet. Put the warm melted butter in a spray bottle and coat the breasts, or use a pastry brush to gently dab the butter onto the tops of the breasts. Place in the oven and bake for 35 to 40 minutes, or until done throughout. Let cool for 5 minutes before serving.

Serves 4 to 6

Nutritional Breakdown: *320 calories, 10 g fat—29% calories from fat, 104 mg cholesterol, 1.5 g fiber, 502 mg sodium*

OLIVE AND FETA STUFFED CHICKEN ROLLS

4 skinless, boneless chicken breast halves (about 1½ pounds), pounded between plastic wrap to ¼ inch thick
Salt and freshly ground black pepper
½ cup dry bread crumbs
1 teaspoon dried oregano
1 large egg white, beaten
½ cup crumbled feta cheese
2 tablespoons finely chopped fresh basil
1 cup packed chopped fresh spinach leaves, stems removed
2 tablespoons finely chopped oil-cured kalamata olives
2 teaspoons unsalted butter, melted

1. Preheat oven to 400°F. Lightly season the chicken breasts with salt and pepper.
2. Combine the bread crumbs, oregano, ¼ teaspoon salt, and ¼ teaspoon pepper in a shallow bowl, and stir to mix well. Transfer to a plate.
3. Place the egg white in a bowl. Dip the chicken breasts in the egg white, allowing the excess to drip back into the bowl. Dredge through the bread crumbs, shaking off any excess. Place the chicken breasts on a flat work surface.
4. In a small mixing bowl, combine the feta, basil, olives, and spinach. Mix with a fork to a pastelike consistency. Divide the stuffing evenly and place in the center of each chicken breast half. Fold in the two sides, and roll up to enclose the stuffing.
5. In a shallow glass baking pan lightly coated with cooking spray, place the chicken breast bundles seam side down, not touching. Using a spray bottle, spray on the melted butter evenly, or use a pastry brush to dab butter on the chicken. Bake for 20 to 25 minutes, or until golden and done throughout. Serve hot or at room temperature.

Serves 4

Nutritional Breakdown: *335 calories, 9.8 g fat—27% calories from fat, 117 mg cholesterol, 1.5 g fiber, 573 mg sodium*

TARRAGON CHICKEN BREASTS WITH ARTICHOKES

En papilotte, an essentially fat-free cooking method, is described on page 52.

4 skinless, boneless chicken breast halves (about 1½ pounds), pounded between plastic wrap to flatten slightly
Salt and freshly ground black pepper
4 tablespoons Defatted Chicken Stock (see page 18)
4 tablespoons dry white wine
1½ tablespoons chopped fresh tarragon, or 2½ teaspoons dried
4 teaspoons unsalted butter, melted
8 large white mushrooms, thinly sliced
2 6-ounce packages frozen artichoke hearts, thawed and bottoms trimmed flat

1. Preheat the oven to 375°F.
2. Place the chicken in a shallow dish and season with salt and pepper. Drizzle on the chicken stock, wine, and tarragon, cover, and marinate for 15 minutes.
3. In a nonstick skillet, heat 1 teaspoon of the butter. Cook the mushrooms over medium heat until their liquid has evaporated, about 5 minutes. Season lightly with salt and pepper. Set aside.
4. Cut 4 15 × 15-inch squares of parchment paper. Fold in half, crease, and open on a flat work surface.
5. In the center of one of the halves place one quarter of the artichokes. Place a chicken breast on the artichokes and top with one quarter of the mushrooms. Drizzle one quarter of the marinade and one quarter of the remaining melted butter over the chicken and vegetables. Season with a grind of pepper.
6. Draw the top flap of the paper over the filling and fold in the edges. Seal the packet with several more narrow folds around the edges. The package should be sealed tightly with the paper still loose to allow for expansion. Repeat to make 4.
7. Place the packets on a baking sheet coated with cooking spray. Bake for 25 to 30 minutes, until the chicken is done and the parchment is puffed. Serve on individual plates and cut at the table.

Serves 4

Nutritional Breakdown: *284 calories, 6.7 g fat—22% calories from fat, 109 mg cholesterol, 5 g fiber, 207 mg sodium*

Sauté

Sautéing is not akin to frying, nor is it like baking, braising, poaching, or grilling. It is a very specific classic French method of cooking in which the food literally jumps around in the pan. Unfortunately, sautéing is seldom associated with low-fat cooking. Traditionally, this method requires food to be cooked with a fairly high dose of heat and with a fairly large dose of butter and/or oil to keep it from sticking to the pan. But the new heavy-gauge nonstick cookware surfaces have rescued this cooking method. And a low-fat sauté made in a nonstick pan offers the same advantages of a quick and delicious classic sauté—namely, a magnificent instant sauce. After the chicken breast is cooked according to the recipe, the evaporated juices and browned flavor bits remaining in the pan can be transformed into a sauce with just a splash of wine, stock, or juice and some seasonings. (See box on next page for complete pan sauce instructions.) The secret of the low-fat sauté is to begin by lightly coating a nonstick pan with vegetable oil cooking spray. This gives the pan a double nonstick coating and reduces to a minimum the amount of butter and/or oil required.

Sautéing Basics for Low-Fat Cooking: Just Jump Right In!

First coat the bottom of a heavy sauté pan lightly with vegetable oil cooking spray. Then add a little butter or oil or a combination of the two and heat the pan over moderately high heat. Let the oil and/or butter come to a fairly high temperature before adding the chicken breasts. First pat the chicken breasts with a paper towel to remove excess moisture, including marinades, then place in the hot pan. Sauté the chicken breasts without moving the pieces around until the underside is nicely browned according to the recipe instructions, or individual taste. Turn, brown the other side, and remove when cooked through (or if the chicken will be returned to the pan later, it should be undercooked at this stage). Now you're ready to make a wonderful pan sauce.

Every Sauté Comes with an Instant Sauce

After the chicken breasts have been browned, the next step is known as deglazing, which is a way of retrieving all the pan juices to create a full-flavored, almost-instant sauce. Remove the cooked chicken breasts from the pan to a platter, cover with foil to keep warm. With the heat still at medium-high, quickly add ¼ to ½ cup stock, wine, or other liquid (such as any remaining marinade) to the pan. Cook, stirring constantly, scraping up any browned particles stuck to the bottom of the pan, until the liquid is reduced to a syrup. Add more liquid and reduce until it forms the desired sauce consistency. No thickener or butter is added to this simple type of sauce. A splash of liqueur, such as brandy, port, Grand Marnier, or vermouth, along with a few tablespoons of fresh chopped herbs can be added as part of the deglazing liquid to enhance the flavor of the sauce. Adjust the seasoning with salt and freshly ground black or white pepper. Place the chicken breasts on plates and drizzle the sauce over them. That's it.

CHICKEN BREASTS WITH CREAMY SPRING ONION SAUCE

Serve this delicious dish with noodles, couscous, or new potatoes with extra nonfat sour cream, chopped parsley, and freshly ground black pepper. Spring onions are a cross between a green onion and an onion; they are mild and flavorful. You can substitute green onions if they aren't available, however.

6 to 8 large spring onions, bulbs only, coarsely chopped
½ cup medium-dry white wine (such as Chablis)
½ cup Rich Chicken Stock (see page 16)
5 to 6 threads saffron, chopped
4 skinless, boneless chicken breast halves (about 1½ pounds)
2 tablespoons fresh lemon juice
2 teaspoons grated lemon zest
1 tablespoon extra-virgin olive oil
2 garlic cloves, minced
Salt and freshly ground white pepper
½ cup low-fat sour cream
2 tablespoons snipped fresh chives

1. In a small saucepan, bring the spring onions, wine, chicken stock, and saffron to a boil and reduce the liquid by half, about 6 minutes. Set the pan aside.

2. Place the chicken in a glass baking dish, and sprinkle on the lemon juice, zest, 2 teaspoons of the oil, and the garlic. Season with salt and pepper. Marinate at room temperature for 30 minutes.

3. Drain the chicken and reserve the marinade. In a large nonstick sauté pan or skillet lightly coated with cooking spray, heat the remaining 1 teaspoon oil. Sauté the chicken over medium-high heat until browned and done, about 5 minutes per side. Transfer the chicken to a platter. Cover with foil to keep warm.

4. In the same pan, bring the marinade and reserved onion mixture to a boil and reduce slightly. Cool, place in a blender with the sour cream, and blend until smooth. Pour into a clean saucepan.

5. Gently rewarm the sauce over medium-low heat and adjust the seasoning with salt and pepper. Arrange the chicken on a platter and spoon on the sauce. Garnish with the chives.

Serves 4

Nutritional Breakdown: *279 calories, 5.6 g fat—18% calories from fat, 98.6 mg cholesterol, 1.1 g fiber, 135 mg sodium*

CHICKEN CAKES WITH BALSAMIC-SHALLOT SAUCE

In addition to the crab boiling spice, and Worcestershire and Tabasco sauces, add Dijon mustard, cilantro, and green onions for a chicken cake taste sensation. These are versatile as main dish or appetizer selections.

8 medium shallots, unpeeled
1 teaspoon extra-virgin olive oil, or more
1 cup dry white wine
1 cup Defatted Chicken Stock (see page 18)
3 tablespoons balsamic vinegar
1 pound ground skinless, boneless chicken breast
3 tablespoons finely chopped celery
2 tablespoons finely chopped onion
3 tablespoons seeded and finely diced red bell pepper
1 tablespoon finely chopped flat-leaf parsley
1 teaspoon grated lemon zest, chopped
1 small garlic clove, finely minced
1½ cups fresh bread crumbs (see page 61)
1 whole large egg plus 1 large egg white, whisked together
1 teaspoon salt
1 teaspoon ground crab boiling spice mix
1 teaspoon Worcestershire sauce
¼ teaspoon Tabasco sauce
1 tablespoon unsalted butter
1 tablespoon canola oil

1. To make the sauce, preheat the oven to 350° F. Drizzle the shallots with the olive oil, wrap tightly in foil, place on a baking sheet, and roast for 45 to 55 minutes, or until tender. Leave the oven on. When cool, peel and chop the shallots.
2. Meanwhile, in a nonreactive medium saucepan, bring the wine, chicken stock, and balsamic vinegar to a boil and reduce to ½ cup, about 15 minutes. Add the shallots and set the pan aside.
3. In a large bowl, combine the chicken, celery, onion, bell pepper, parsley, lemon zest, and garlic and mix well with your hands or a wooden spoon. Stir in 1 cup of the bread crumbs, the egg and egg white, salt, crab boiling spice, Worcestershire, and Tabasco until well combined.
4. Cover with plastic wrap and chill for 1 hour. Divide the mixture into 8 portions and flatten to form cakes. Sprinkle the remaining bread crumbs on all sides and pat into the cakes.
5. In a large nonstick sauté pan or skil-

let lightly coated with cooking spray, heat the butter and canola oil. Sauté the chicken breast cakes 4 at a time over medium heat until browned, about 3 minutes per side.

6. Place the chicken cakes in a single layer in a baking dish. Bake for 10 to 12 minutes, or until done throughout.

7. Meanwhile, reheat the sauce, spoon even amounts of the sauce onto 4 warmed plates, and nestle the chicken cakes into the shallots and sauce.

Serves 4

Nutritional Breakdown: *448 calories, 12.8 g fat—26% calories from fat, 127 mg cholesterol, 2.2 g fiber, 1,476 mg sodium*

CHICKEN PAILLARDS WITH MUSHROOMS AND PEPPERS

A paillard is a cutlet or flattened piece of meat—in this case, chicken breast. It is a particularly elegant way of portioning this food, and can be the basis for many variations. Paillards can be served with lemon sauce, with shiitake mushrooms, with a light, fresh Tomato-Herb Sauce (see page 40), or with a ragout of fresh spring vegetables.

2 tablespoons seasoned dry bread crumbs
1 teaspoon dried herbs of choice (such as oregano, thyme, basil, and rosemary)
Salt and freshly ground black pepper
4 skinless, boneless chicken breast halves (about 1½ pounds), pounded between plastic wrap to ¼ inch thick
1 tablespoon extra-virgin olive oil
2 garlic cloves, minced
½ pound white mushrooms, stems removed and caps sliced
⅔ cup Defatted Chicken Stock (see page 18)
1 medium red bell pepper, seeded and cut into strips
2 teaspoons fresh lemon juice
¼ teaspoon crushed red pepper
2 teaspoons cornstarch, dissolved in 2 tablespoons chicken stock
2 tablespoons coarsely chopped flat-leaf parsley

1. Combine the bread crumbs, ½ teaspoon of the dried herbs, and a pinch of salt and pepper and sprinkle over the chicken paillards, pressing slightly but being careful not to tear the thin breast meat.

2. In a large nonstick sauté pan or skillet lightly coated with cooking spray, heat the oil. Add the chicken breasts and sauté for 1 to 2 minutes per side over medium-high heat. Do not overcook. Place on a platter and cover with foil to keep warm.

3. To the same skillet, add the garlic and sauté over medium heat for 2 to 3 minutes. Do not let the garlic turn brown. Add the mushrooms and cook until most of the liquid has evaporated, about 5 minutes. Add 1 tablespoon of the chicken stock and the bell pepper and sauté over medium-high heat for 3 minutes, or until the moisture has evaporated.

4. Add the remaining stock, the lemon juice, the remaining ½ teaspoon dried herbs, and the crushed red pepper and reduce the heat to low. Stir the cornstarch mixture into the sauce and cook, partially covered, until the peppers are tender and the sauce is thickened slightly, about 7 to 8 minutes.

5. To assemble, briefly rewarm the chicken breasts and sauce, being careful not to overcook. Spoon the sauce over the chicken paillards. Sprinkle with the chopped parsley.

Serves 4

Nutritional Breakdown: *266 calories, 6.2 g fat—22% calories from fat, 98.6 mg cholesterol, 1.3 g fiber, 294 mg sodium*

Vegetable Oil Cooking Spray Has Surfaced . . . Again!

It's been around for a long time. However, in the days of cooking with plenty of butter and oil, it was simply an ingredient that was pushed to the back of the cupboard or used by people on special diets. Now, it's shelved front and center in the supermarket, available everywhere, and is more specifically designed for the needs of those of us who are cooking lighter, low-fat fare. Oils under pressure now include canola, corn, and olive. And, if you spray just a touch on the grill top the chicken breast doesn't stick. The aerosol spray container distributes the oil in a very fine and even spray over the cooking surface. It is even possible to create your own: buy a plastic spray bottle with a very fine spray (like the ones you use to mist your ferns) and fill it with the oil you use most frequently—olive, canola, peanut, or light sesame oil.

CHICKEN BREASTS WITH TOMATO AND BASIL SAUCE ON LINGUINE

This extra-fresh, healthful, and quick-to-make sauce is known as a "crude" sauce because it is uncooked. You can sauté a tablespoon of finely diced Italian bacon, a bit of minced onion, some red pepper flakes, and 1 teaspoon of garlic-infused olive oil and add it to the sauce at the end. Another version is a cooked sauce. You can add a splash of white wine to 2 to 3 cups of this sauce and heat and serve over linguine with a shaving of fresh Parmesan.

2 cups coarsely chopped, peeled, and seeded plum tomatoes
1½ tablespoons extra-virgin olive oil
¼ cup finely chopped fresh basil
2 tablespoons finely chopped flat-leaf parsley
3 tablespoons minced white onion
Salt and freshly ground black pepper
¾ pound dried linguine
1 tablespoon unsalted butter
4 skinless, boneless chicken breast halves (about 1½ pounds), pounded between plastic wrap to ½ inch thick
2 tablespoons dry white wine
2 teaspoons drained and rinsed capers, coarsely chopped
Parsley sprigs for garnish

1. To make the sauce, in a small bowl, toss together the tomatoes, 1 tablespoon of the oil, the basil, parsley, onion, and salt and pepper to taste. Set aside.

2. In a large stockpot, bring lightly salted water to a boil. Cook the linguine to al dente. Drain and keep warm.

3. Meanwhile, in a large nonstick sauté pan or skillet lightly coated with cooking spray, heat the butter and the remaining ½ tablespoon oil. Sauté the chicken breasts over medium-high heat until browned, about 3 to 4 minutes per side. Add the wine and capers and cook, partially covered, for 3 to 4 minutes more, or until the chicken breasts are done. Slice the chicken breasts on the diagonal into ¼-inch-thick pieces.

4. To assemble, place the hot pasta in a large warmed pasta bowl, toss with the tomato sauce, and serve in 4 individual bowls. Place slices of chicken on each serving and garnish with the parsley.

Serves 4

Nutritional Breakdown: *602 calories, 11.8 g fat—18% calories from fat, 106 mg cholesterol, 3.2 g fiber, 179 mg sodium*

CHICKEN NIÇOISE SALAD

Chicken breast "fillets," which are delicate strips of nonfat white-meat chicken, can be substituted in this recipe. Sold often as "chicken tenders," each one is about an individual bite. Remove the tendon and reduce the cooking time as these morsels cook very quickly.

Haricots verts, as they are called in France, are a very slender green bean.

Dressing

2 anchovy fillets packed in olive oil, well drained and rinsed, 2 teaspoons of anchovy oil reserved
½ cup extra-virgin olive oil
¼ cup Defatted Chicken Stock (see page 18)
3 tablespoons red wine vinegar
2 garlic cloves, peeled and chopped
1 teaspoon chopped fresh rosemary
½ teaspoon freshly ground black pepper

Salad

4 skinless, boneless chicken breast halves (about 1½ pounds)
Salt and freshly ground black pepper
1 teaspoon canola or other vegetable oil
10 small red potatoes, well scrubbed
½ pound French haricots verts (or regular green beans)
1 small red onion, cut into very thin rings
12 cups mixed lettuce (such as mâche, mixed baby lettuces, romaine, or Boston)
12 or more tiny niçoise olives
4 hard-boiled eggs, halved
12 cherry tomatoes, halved
1 tablespoon capers, drained

1. To make the dressing, in a blender or the bowl of a food processor fitted with the metal blade, combine the anchovy fillets, the 2 teaspoons of reserved anchovy oil, the olive oil, chicken stock, vinegar, garlic, rosemary, and pepper and process until smooth. Transfer to a bowl and let stand.

2. Place the chicken breasts in a single layer on a plate. Drizzle on 2 tablespoons of the dressing and coat well. Season with a scant amount of salt and pepper. Marinate for 10 minutes.

3. In a large nonstick sauté pan or skillet, heat the 1 teaspoon of vegetable oil. Sauté the chicken until lightly browned and done, about 4 to 5 minutes per side. Place on paper towels to remove any excess oil. Let cool to room temperature. Slice on the diagonal into ¼-inch-thick pieces.

4. Meanwhile, place the potatoes in a large saucepan or stockpot with enough water to cover completely. Boil just until tender, about 12 to 15 minutes, remove with a slotted spoon, and reserve the boiling water. Cool the potatoes, cut in quarters, and set aside.

5. Add the green beans to the boiling water, reduce the heat to a simmer, and cook to crisp-tender, about 1 minute for the haricots verts, or 3 minutes for regular green beans. Do not overcook. Drain and run cold water over the beans. Place in a mixing bowl and set aside.

6. To assemble the salad, place the red onion and lettuces in a large mixing bowl. Drizzle 2 to 3 tablespoons of the dressing over the onion rings and lettuces and toss to mix well. Make a layer on a large serving platter. Add the green beans to the mixing bowl. Toss lightly with 1 tablespoon of the dressing. Arrange in a mound on the lettuce. Repeat with the potato wedges and another tablespoon of dressing, and add a scant amount of salt and pepper. Place the chicken slices in the center, and arrange the olives, hard-boiled eggs, and tomatoes around the chicken and sprinkle on the capers. Drizzle 1 tablespoon of dressing over the egg halves. Serve the remaining dressing on the side, if desired, and pass the pepper mill.

Serves 8

Nutritional Breakdown (includes 2 teaspoons of dressing per serving): *344 calories, 11.2 g fat—29% calories from fat, 50.2 mg cholesterol, 5.4 g fiber, 177 mg sodium*

Picking Herbs and Aromatics for Flavorful Sautés

Chicken breasts, herbs, and spices can be partnered in many ways. Lots of shallots and garlic show up in the sauté pan. Fresh basil, marjoram, flat-leaf parsley (with better character than curly parsley), sage, oregano, thyme, tarragon, cilantro, dill, rosemary, and chives are all high on the list. Fresh herbs should be selected over dried if possible since the cooking time is so short and the fresh garden flavors are more delicate. When dried are used, use half the amount of fresh.

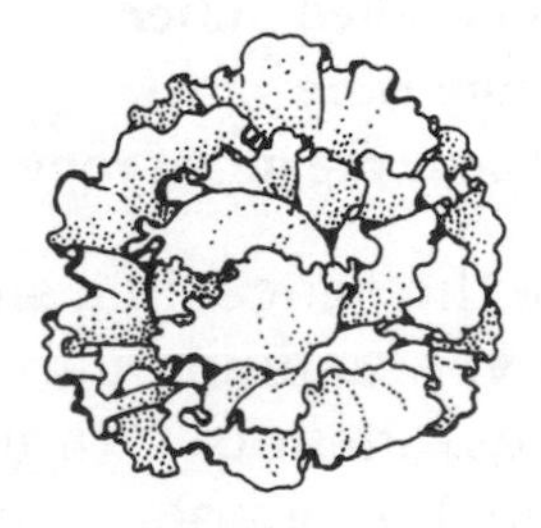

SAUTÉED CHICKEN WITH TARRAGON-TOMATO SAUCE

No need to strain this sauce which looks very appealing with flecks of tomato and fresh tarragon.

Sauce

2 ripe plum tomatoes, peeled, seeded, and finely chopped
3 shallots, finely chopped
2 tablespoons chopped fresh tarragon, plus 1 tablespoon for garnish
½ teaspoon freshly ground black pepper
¼ cup tarragon wine vinegar
3 drops Worcestershire sauce

Chicken Breasts

4 skinless, boneless chicken breast halves (about 1½ pounds)
Salt and freshly ground black pepper
1 tablespoon unsalted butter
⅔ cup dry white wine
1 cup low-fat sour cream, at room temperature

1. To make the sauce, in a small saucepan over medium-high heat, cook the tomatoes, shallots, 2 tablespoons of the tarragon, the pepper, vinegar, and Worcestershire until only about 2 to 3 tablespoons of liquid remain, about 10 minutes. Set the pan aside.

2. Lightly season the chicken breasts with salt and pepper. In a large nonstick sauté pan or skillet lightly coated with cooking spray, melt the butter. Sauté the chicken over medium-high heat for about 2 to 3 minutes per side, or just until lightly browned. Do not overcook. Remove the chicken breasts to a platter.

3. Deglaze the pan with the wine, and reduce over high heat by half. Add the tomato mixture and the chicken to the pan and cook, partially covered, over low heat, just until the chicken is done, about 3 to 4 minutes.

4. Remove the pan from the heat and place the breasts on 4 individual plates. Cover to keep warm. Stir the sour cream into the tomato mixture and, over low heat, rewarm the sauce. Spoon the sauce on the chicken and garnish with the remaining 1 tablespoon chopped tarragon.

Serves 4

Nutritional Breakdown: *297calories, 5.2 g fat—16% calories from fat, 106 mg cholesterol, 0.5 g fiber, 165 mg sodium*

SAUTÉED CHICKEN BREASTS WITH FRUITY COCONUT-CURRY SAUCE

Sauce

1 tablespoon unsalted butter
½ cup minced onion
1 peeled green apple, cored and grated
1 cup crushed fresh pineapple
2 tablespoons all-purpose flour
1 tablespoon Madras curry powder, or more to taste
1 teaspoon salt
1 teaspoon sugar
1 tablespoon fresh lemon juice
½ teaspoon finely minced fresh peeled ginger
2 tablespoons unsweetened shredded coconut
1 cup coconut milk
1 cup Defatted Chicken Stock (see page 18)

Chicken Breasts

1 tablespoon unsalted butter
1 medium yellow onion, quartered
1 tablespoon dried herbs (such as sage, savory, parsley, and basil)
4 skinless, boneless chicken breast halves (about 1½ pounds), pounded between plastic wrap to flatten slightly
Salt and freshly ground black pepper
¼ cup dry white wine or Defatted Chicken Stock (see page 18)
2 tablespoons Major Grey's chutney, chopped

1. To make the sauce, in a medium nonstick sauté pan lightly coated with cooking spray, heat the butter. Sauté the onion until tender. Add the apple and pineapple and cook for 2 minutes more. Sprinkle in the flour, curry powder, salt, sugar, lemon juice, ginger, and coconut and stir to combine. Stir in the coconut milk and the chicken stock until well mixed, and cook over very low heat about 30 minutes, until the sauce thickens. Let cool slightly. Transfer to a blender and blend until smooth.
2. In a large nonstick sauté pan or skillet lightly coated with cooking spray, heat the butter. Sauté the onion over medium-high heat until tender. Sprinkle on the dried herbs and cook for 1 minute more. Transfer to a bowl and set aside. Season the chicken with salt and pepper.
3. In the same pan, sauté the chicken

breasts over medium-high heat until lightly browned on both sides, about 3 to 4 minutes. Transfer the chicken breasts to a plate.

4. Deglaze the pan with the white wine, and reduce the liquid by half, about 3 minutes. Stir in the onions and the chutney. Return the chicken and curry sauce to the pan, and cook 3 to 4 minutes more over low heat, or until the chicken is done and the sauce is thick. Serve immediately.

Serves 4 to 6

Nutritional Breakdown: *358 calories, 8.6 g fat—22% calories from fat, 109 mg cholesterol, 3.6 g fiber, 934 mg sodium*

GOAT CHEESE AND BASIL STUFFED CHICKEN BREASTS

To change the personality of this dish from Provençal to Southwestern, substitute cilantro for the basil and add a little minced jalapeño to the tomatoes along with diced red onion.

4 skinless, boneless chicken breast halves (about 1½ pounds), pounded between plastic wrap to ⅓ inch thick
Salt and freshly ground black pepper
4 tablespoons goat cheese
3 teaspoons unsalted butter
1 teaspoon chopped fresh thyme leaves, or ½ teaspoon dried
12 chiffonade-cut fresh basil leaves, plus 1 tablespoon chopped fresh basil
2 tablespoons chopped fresh chives
2 large ripe tomatoes, seeded and finely diced
¼ teaspoon dried thyme
2 tablespoons white wine vinegar, preferably thyme scented
2 tablespoons extra-virgin olive oil
2 cups torn salad greens (such as baby lettuce, curly endive, and radicchio)

1. Place the chicken breasts on a flat work surface. Lightly season with salt and pepper on both sides.

2. In a small bowl, combine the goat cheese, 2 teaspoons of the butter, the thyme leaves, basil chiffonade, 1 tablespoon of the chives, and a pinch of salt and pepper. Mix with a fork to form a paste. Place equal amounts of the stuffing mixture in the center of each chicken breast. Fold the ends in, as if wrapping a package, to cover the stuffing. Set aside, seam sides down.

3. In a medium bowl, combine the tomatoes, the 1 tablespoon chopped basil, and the dried thyme and drizzle on the vinegar and 1 tablespoon of the oil. Gently toss to combine. Season with salt and pepper to taste. Set aside to marinate.

4. In a large nonstick sauté pan or skillet lightly coated with cooking spray, heat the remaining 1 teaspoon butter and the remaining 1 tablespoon oil. Sauté the chicken breasts seam sides down over medium-high heat until browned, about 2 to 3 minutes per side. Reduce the heat, partially cover the pan, and cook for 5 minutes more, seam sides down, or until the chicken is done. Remove the pan from the heat. Gently remove the chicken breasts and set aside to cool slightly.

5. On 4 individual serving plates, place the salad greens around the outer edges of the plates. Drain the tomatoes, reserving the marinade, and divide among the plates. Drizzle the reserved marinade over the lettuce leaves. Slice the chicken breasts on the diagonal and gently place overlapping chicken slices on top of the tomatoes. Garnish with the remaining 1 tablespoon chopped chives.

Serves 4

Nutritional Breakdown: *272 calories, 8.7 g fat—[illegible] calories from fat, 105 mg cholesterol, 1.1 g fiber, 161 mg sodium*

An Update on Sautéing Pans

Investing in a set of nonstick pans is a great idea. However, if you need only one or two to suit your cooking style, select a 10- to 12-inch nonstick heavy-gauge sauté pan and a slightly larger skillet. The skillet should have a tight-fitting cover. Reducing the amount of butter and oil required to keep food from sticking to the surface of the pan makes your cooking more healthful, no matter what you whip up.

SAUTÉED CHICKEN BREASTS WITH 20 SHALLOTS

This may sound like an awful lot of shallots, but they mellow and sweeten when cooked. Serve with grilled bread, white or brown rice, pasta, or something a little more exotic like couscous or quinoa.

When igniting the liquor, use a long match, and keep your face, hair, and clothing clear of the flame.

1 tablespoon extra-virgin olive oil
1 teaspoon unsalted butter
4 skinless, boneless chicken breast halves (about 1½ pounds)
Salt and freshly ground white pepper
20 small shallots, peeled and chopped
2 large garlic cloves, peeled and finely minced
¼ cup best-quality Cognac
2 medium ripe tomatoes, peeled, seeded, and chopped

1. Lightly coat a large nonstick sauté pan or skillet with a tight-fitting cover with cooking spray, and then heat the oil and butter. Season the chicken with salt and pepper and sauté until lightly browned, about 2 to 3 minutes per side. Add the shallots and garlic and shake the pan so that the shallots line the bottom.

2. Cover the sauté pan, reduce the heat, and continue cooking until the shallots are tender and the chicken breasts are done, about 8 to 10 minutes. Transfer the chicken to a serving platter and keep warm.

3. Meanwhile, in a small saucepan, warm the Cognac and pour it into the sauté pan. Then stand back and carefully ignite the Cognac. Let it burn off, shaking the pan during the process. Quickly stir in the tomatoes, mixing into the shallots, cover the pan, and cook for 2 to 3 minutes more over low heat, or just until the tomatoes are done. Pour over the chicken and serve immediately.

Serves 4

Nutritional Breakdown: *335 calories, 6.7 g fat—19% calories from fat, 101 mg cholesterol, 1.3 g fiber, 130 mg sodium*

LEMON-THYME CHICKEN BREASTS

This chicken is very lemony, the way I like it! I use the juice of all 5 lemons, but as few as 3 will produce a memorable taste.

4 skinless, boneless chicken breast halves (about 1½ pounds), pounded between plastic wrap to flatten slightly
Juice of 5 lemons, or to taste
1 tablespoon grated lemon zest
Salt and freshly ground white pepper
2 tablespoons vermouth
1 cup Chardonnay or other dry white wine
2 medium garlic cloves, finely minced
5 tablespoons chopped shallots
2 tablespoons minced fresh thyme, or 1 tablespoon dried
1½ teaspoons extra-virgin olive oil
1½ teaspoons unsalted butter
1 teaspoon cornstarch, dissolved in 1 tablespoon cold water

1. Place the chicken breasts on a deep plate in a single layer. In a bowl, combine the lemon juice, zest, salt and pepper, vermouth, wine, garlic, 4 tablespoons of the shallots, and the thyme. Pour the mixture over the chicken, cover tightly with plastic wrap, and marinate for 2 hours in the refrigerator.

2. Drain off the marinade and reserve. Pat the chicken breasts dry with paper towels, scraping any shallots and garlic pieces back into the marinade. In a large nonstick sauté pan or skillet lightly coated with cooking spray, heat the oil and the butter. Sauté the chicken breasts until lightly browned and done, about 3 to 4 minutes per side. Transfer to a platter and cover with foil to keep warm.

3. Combine the cornstarch mixture with ¼ cup of the reserved marinade. Set aside.

4. To the sauté pan, add the remaining marinade. Over high heat, reduce by half, about 6 minutes. Add the cornstarch mixture, stir to mix well, and cook for 5 minutes, or until the sauce thickens. Place the chicken breasts on 4 individual plates and spoon on the sauce. Top with the reserved 1 tablespoon chopped shallots.

Serves 4

Nutritional Breakdown: *304 calories, 5.4 g fat—16% calories from fat, 102 mg cholesterol, 0.8 g fiber, 119 mg sodium*

CHAMPAGNE AND CHANTERELLE CHICKEN BREASTS

4 skinless, boneless chicken breast halves (about 1½ pounds)
Salt and freshly ground white pepper
2 tablespoons unsalted butter
2 tablespoons olive oil
2 shallots, chopped
1 small garlic clove, finely minced
1 cup Champagne
1 cup Rich Chicken Stock (see page 16)
¾ pound chanterelle mushrooms, washed, trimmed, and quartered
1 teaspoon cornstarch, dissolved in 1 tablespoon chicken stock
1 cup low-fat sour cream

1. Preheat the oven to 200° F. Season the chicken breasts with salt and pepper.
2. In a large nonstick sauté pan or skillet lightly coated with cooking spray, heat 1 tablespoon of the butter and 1 tablespoon of the oil. Sauté the chicken over medium-high heat until browned, about 5 minutes per side. Remove the chicken from the pan to foil and pat with paper towels to remove any excess fat. Cover the chicken with the foil and set in the warm oven.
3. Cook the shallots and garlic until tender, about 1 to 2 minutes. Add the Champagne and ½ cup of the chicken stock and boil until the liquid is reduced by half, about 3 to 4 minutes, then set aside.
4. In a medium pan, heat the remaining 1 tablespoon butter and 1 tablespoon oil. Sauté the chanterelles over medium-high heat until tender, about 4 to 5 minutes. Add the remaining ½ cup stock and cook about 3 to 4 minutes, until most of the moisture has evaporated. Transfer to a bowl and cover to keep warm.
5. Return the pan with the Champagne and shallots to medium heat and stir in the cornstarch mixture. Cook, stirring constantly, until the sauce is slightly thickened, about 2 to 3 minutes. Over very low heat, stir in the sour cream, season with salt and pepper, add the mushrooms, and heat through.
6. Place the chicken breasts on a large, deep platter. Pour the sauce and mushrooms over the chicken and serve.

Serves 4

Nutritional Breakdown: *374 calories, 9.3 g fat—23% calories from fat, 107 mg cholesterol, 9.3 g fiber, 526 mg sodium*

CHICKEN WITH GRAPEFRUIT, RED ONION, AND RADICCHIO

4 skinless, boneless chicken breast halves (about 1½ pounds), pounded between plastic wrap to ⅓ inch thick
Salt and freshly ground white pepper
1 tablespoon grated grapefruit zest
¾ cup dry white wine
1 tablespoon dry vermouth
¼ teaspoon dry mustard
2 tablespoons unsalted butter
3 medium red onions, halved and thinly sliced
1 cup fresh pink grapefruit juice
2 teaspoons honey
1 teaspoon dried thyme
1 medium head radicchio (about ½ pound), cut into chiffonade
1 pink grapefruit, sectioned and membranes removed, trimmed

1. Season the chicken breasts with salt and pepper and place in a glass baking dish. In a bowl, mix together the grapefruit zest, ½ cup of the wine, the vermouth, and the dry mustard. Drizzle over the chicken breasts, cover tightly with plastic wrap, and marinate for 1 hour.
2. In a large nonstick sauté pan or skillet lightly coated with cooking spray, heat 1 tablespoon of the butter. Add the red onions and sauté until tender over medium heat. Increase the heat, cover, and cook, stirring frequently, until the onions caramelize, about 8 to 10 minutes. Transfer to a bowl and set aside.
3. To the same skillet, melt the remaining 1 tablespoon butter. Remove the chicken, pat dry, and discard the marinade. Sauté the chicken over medium-high heat until lightly browned and done, about 3 to 4 minutes per side. Remove and slice in ½-inch strips and cover with foil to keep warm.
4. Add the grapefruit juice to the pan and cook over medium heat until reduced by half, about 5 minutes. Add the remaining ¼ cup wine, the honey, and the thyme to the pan and, over high heat, reduce until only about 3 tablespoons remain, about 7 minutes. Lower the heat to medium-high, add the radicchio, and cook just until wilted, about 4 minutes. Remove from the pan with a slotted spoon. Add the grapefruit sections and gently heat through, about 2 minutes. Transfer to a dish and keep warm.
5. Over high heat, reduce the liquid in the skillet to about 2 tablespoons, about

2 minutes more. Make a bed of radicchio on 4 individual plates, top with chicken strips, drizzle on a bit of pan sauce, and top with the caramelized onions. Garnish around the sides with the grapefruit sections.

Serves 4

Nutritional Breakdown: *376 calories, 8.5 g fat—20% calories from fat, 114 mg cholesterol, 2.5 g fiber, 179 mg sodium*

GLAZED CHICKEN BREASTS WITH PEACH CHUTNEY

3 large ripe peaches, peeled and chopped
1 medium yellow onion, finely chopped
Salt and freshly ground white pepper
1 cinnamon stick, broken in 4 pieces
½ cup fresh orange juice
¼ cup fresh lemon juice
1 teaspoon grated orange zest
1 teaspoon grated lemon zest
½ teaspoon plus pinch ground ginger
4 skinless, boneless chicken breast halves (about 1½ pounds)
1½ teaspoons unsalted butter
1½ teaspoons extra-virgin olive oil
2 teaspoons honey
2 tablespoons red wine vinegar
2 tablespoons white wine

1. In a large bowl, combine the peaches, onion, a scant amount of salt and pepper, the cinnamon stick, orange and lemon juices, both zests, and ½ teaspoon ground ginger. Stir to combine. Add the chicken breasts and cover well with the peach mixture. Cover with plastic wrap and marinate in the refrigerator for 2 hours.

2. Preheat the oven to 300°F.

3. Remove the chicken from the marinade, scrape off any peaches back into the bowl, and pat off any excess. Reserve the marinade.

4. In a large nonstick sauté pan or skillet lightly coated with cooking spray, heat the butter and oil. Sprinkle a pinch of ginger into the pan and sauté the breasts over medium-high heat until browned, about 5 to 6 minutes. Increase the heat to high and when very hot, drizzle in the honey. Toss the chicken in the honey to coat and cook for about

1 minute more. Transfer the chicken to a baking pan and place in the oven, set on low, uncovered, and continue cooking until done through.

5. To the pan, add the vinegar and white wine, and reduce slightly over high heat, scraping up the browned bits. Add the reserved peach marinade. Cook over medium heat for about 6 to 8 minutes, or until the peaches are tender and the liquid is evaporated. Remove and discard the cinnamon pieces. Serve the chicken with equal amounts of hot peach chutney on the side.

Serves 4

Nutritional Breakdown: *321 calories, 5.5 g fat—16% calories from fat, 102 mg cholesterol, 3.5 g fiber, 113 mg sodium*

CHICKEN WITH BASIL, ENDIVE, AND PEPPERS

1 tablespoon extra-virgin olive oil
4 large Belgian endives, trimmed and sliced into ½-inch-thick pieces
2 garlic cloves, very thinly sliced
2 tablespoons Defatted Chicken Stock (see page 18), drained
Salt and freshly ground white pepper
4 skinless, boneless chicken breast halves (about 1½ pounds)
¼ cup packed chiffonade-cut fresh basil leaves
¼ cup fresh lemon juice
2 cups torn baby curly-leaf endive
1 red bell pepper, roasted, peeled, seeded, and cut into julienne (see Note)
1 yellow bell pepper, roasted, peeled, seeded, and cut into julienne (see Note)
1½ teaspoons white wine vinegar
1½ teaspoons balsamic vinegar

1. In a large nonstick sauté pan or skillet lightly coated with cooking spray, heat 1 teaspoon of the oil. Cook the Belgian endive over medium heat for 2 to 3 minutes, stirring occasionally. Stir in the garlic, chicken stock, and a pinch of salt and pepper and continue cooking, partially covered, until the endive is tender but still holds its shape, about 1 to 2 minutes more. Transfer to a large mixing bowl.

2. To the same pan, add 1 teaspoon of the oil. Lightly season the chicken breasts with salt and pepper and sauté until browned and done, about 4 to 5 minutes per side.

3. Transfer the chicken to a cutting board, and slice thin on the diagonal. Add the chicken to the bowl with the Belgian endive. Add the basil, drizzle on the lemon juice, and toss to mix well. Adjust the seasoning with salt and pepper to taste. Set aside.

4. In a large mixing bowl, combine the curly-leaf endive and the bell pepper strips. In a jar with a tight-fitting lid, combine the remaining 1 teaspoon oil and the white wine and balsamic vinegars. Drizzle on the endive and peppers and toss to coat well.

5. Divide the curly endive and peppers among 4 plates. Top with the mixture of chicken and Belgian endive. Pass the pepper mill.

Serves 4

Note: To roast peppers: Broil the peppers under direct heat for about 5 minutes, turning frequently. When the skins have blackened, allow to cool slightly, then peel the loosened skin away from the peppers. Remove the seeds and cut.

Nutritional Breakdown: *261 calories, 5.8 g fat—21% calories from fat, 98.6 mg cholesterol, 3.3 g fiber, 132 mg sodium*

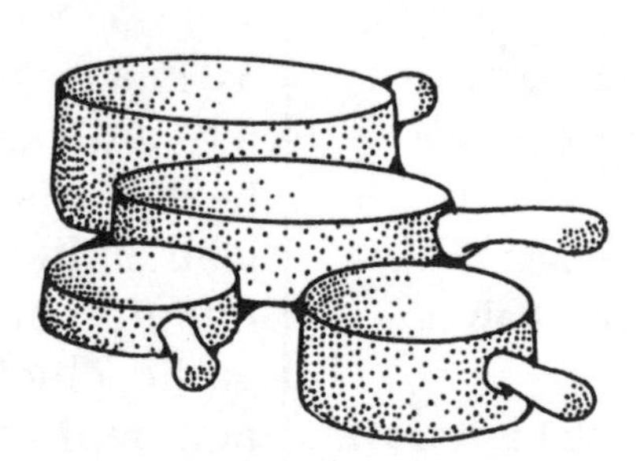

CHICKEN PAILLARDS WITH WALNUTS AND PARSLEY SAUCE

4 skinless, boneless chicken breast halves (about 1½ pounds), pounded between plastic wrap to ¼ inch thick
Salt and freshly ground white pepper
⅓ cup toasted chopped walnuts
¼ cup all-purpose flour
3 tablespoons finely minced parsley, plus 1 teaspoon for garnish
½ teaspoon minced garlic
1 teaspoon unsalted butter
1 teaspoon extra-virgin olive oil
1 cup dry white wine

1. Preheat the oven to 200° F.
2. Season the chicken breasts with salt and pepper.
3. In a blender or food processor fitted with the metal blade, process three-quarters of the walnuts to a powder. Mix with the flour and a pinch of salt and pepper. Spread evenly on a double sheet of wax paper.
4. In a small bowl, combine 2 tablespoons of the parsley, the remaining walnuts, and the garlic and set aside.
5. Dredge the chicken breasts in the flour mixture, shaking off any excess.
6. In a large nonstick sauté pan or skillet lightly coated with cooking spray, heat half of the butter and half of the oil. Sauté 2 of the chicken paillards over medium heat until lightly browned, about 1 to 2 minutes per side. Place on a baking sheet, covered, in the oven, set on low, to keep warm. Repeat with the remaining butter, oil, and 2 chicken paillards.
7. Add the wine and deglaze the pan, scraping up all the brown bits, until the liquid is slightly reduced. Add the reserved walnut-parsley mixture. Continue to cook until reduced to ½ cup, about 3 minutes. Drizzle the sauce over the paillards and layer them, overlapping, on a platter. Dust the top with the remaining teaspoon of parsley.

Serves 4

Nutritional Breakdown: *340 calories, 10.5 g fat—28% calories from fat, 101 mg cholesterol, 0.9 g fiber, 117 mg sodium*

CLASSIC ROSEMARY CHICKEN SALAD

Place a scoop of this salad on a bed of lettuce with a dusting of chopped walnuts, or use it to fill two pieces of reduced-calorie bread, in which case you may want to serve the grapes on the side.

1 tablespoon plus 1 teaspoon extra-virgin olive oil
1 small garlic clove, minced
4 skinless, boneless chicken breast halves (about 1½ pounds)
4½ teaspoons finely chopped fresh rosemary
Salt and freshly ground black pepper
⅓ cup dry white wine
⅓ cup Defatted Chicken Stock (see page 18)
1 stalk celery, very thinly sliced
2 green onions, white and green parts, thinly sliced
1 cup seedless red or green grapes, halved
¼ cup reduced-fat mayonnaise or plain nonfat yogurt
¼ cup low-fat or nonfat sour cream
2 teaspoons fresh lemon juice
1–2 tablespoons toasted, finely chopped walnuts for garnish

1. In a medium nonstick sauté pan or skillet, heat the oil and garlic over medium heat for 1 minute. Add the chicken and sauté until browned, about 3 minutes per side. Sprinkle on 1 teaspoon of the rosemary and a scant amount of salt and pepper, and continue to sauté.
2. Add the wine and chicken stock, partially cover, and simmer until the chicken is done, about 5 minutes. Let the chicken cool in the pan juices.
3. Remove the chicken breasts from the pan and chop into bite-size chunks.
4. In a medium mixing bowl, combine the chopped chicken, celery, green onions, and grape halves. Set aside.
5. In the bowl of a mini food processor, combine the mayonnaise, sour cream, lemon juice, the remaining 3½ teaspoons rosemary, and salt and pepper to taste. Process until well combined.
6. Fold the dressing into the chicken until the chicken pieces are well coated. Dust with the walnuts before serving.

Serves 4

Nutritional Breakdown: *311 calories, 8.2 g fat—25% calories from fat, 98.9 mg cholesterol, 0.9 g fiber, 208 mg sodium*

Stir-Fry

When I say "wok" do you think "Chinese food"? Well, in this, the era of low-fat cuisine, woks have become multicultural cooking utensils, stirring up Mexican and Mediterranean as easily as a beloved Kung Pow Chicken. And when it comes to reorienting (no pun intended) our traditional cooking methods to lower fat, stir-frying offers a couple of very specific advantages: a short cooking time, which allows food to retain much of its natural flavor and moisture, and the limited need for oil since the food is literally tossed to and fro on the already slippery surface of the wok to keep it from sticking.

Stir-fry cooking was invented in a time when little firewood was available. In order to intensify the taste of wok-cooked foods, instant flavorings and seasonings were used, such as soy sauce, hoisin, chili-garlic paste, and ginger. So, when cooking low fat with this high-heat quick method, seek out ingredients with an intrinsic kick: balsamic vinegar, infused oils, reduced and concentrated stocks or liquids, intensely flavored wines (like sherry), herbs, garlic, and citrus zests that explode with flavor, as well as vegetables like green onions and bell peppers for the advantage of instant cooking.

Another thing to consider: Always set the table before you begin tossing the food around in the wok, since when a chicken stir-fry is ready, you'd better be, too!

JAPANESE STIR-FRY WITH PEAS

Pea shoots include the leaves and tendrils. They are a taste treat and very interesting visually. Look for pea shoots at an open-air farmers' market during the summer months.

4 skinless, boneless chicken breast halves (about 1½ pounds), pounded slightly between plastic wrap and cut into ½-inch strips
1 tablespoon dark sesame oil
2 large garlic cloves, minced
1 tablespoon minced peeled fresh ginger
¼ teaspoon crushed red pepper
3 tablespoons reduced-sodium soy sauce or tamari
2 teaspoons cornstarch, dissolved in 2 tablespoons water
½ cup Defatted Chicken Stock (see page 18)
¼ cup rice wine vinegar
1 tablespoon honey
1 tablespoon light sesame oil
6 green onions, white and green parts, cut into 1-inch pieces
½ red bell pepper, seeded and cut into julienne
1 pound sugar snap peas, including tendrils and leaves, if possible
¾ pound buckwheat soba noodles, cooked in lightly salted water according to package directions, tossed with 1 tablespoon dark sesame oil, hot

1. In a medium mixing bowl, combine the chicken strips, dark sesame oil, garlic, ginger, pepper, and 1 tablespoon of the soy sauce. Toss to coat the pieces well. Marinate for 15 minutes.
2. In a small bowl, whisk together the cornstarch mixture, chicken stock, the remaining 2 tablespoons soy sauce, the vinegar, and honey.
3. In a wok, heat the light sesame oil. Add the chicken strips, reserving the marinade, and stir-fry over medium-high heat until lightly browned, about 2 to 3 minutes. Add the green onions, bell pepper, and a little of the marinade and stir-fry for 1 minute more. Add the remaining marinade and the stock mixture and bring to a boil, cooking for 2 to 3 minutes, until the chicken strips are done and the sauce thickens. In the last 1 minute of cooking time, add the sugar snap peas and cook until just wilted.
4. Place the noodles in a bowl. Top with the chicken, peas, and sauce, and toss. Serve immediately.

Serves 4

Nutritional Breakdown: *510 calories, 13 g fat—23% calories from fat, 98.6 mg cholesterol, 4.4 g fiber, 1,003 mg sodium*

THAI CHICKEN BREAST STIR-FRY

½ cup Defatted Chicken Stock (see page 18)
1 tablespoon fresh lime juice
2 teaspoons cornstarch, dissolved in 1½ tablespoons soy sauce
2 teaspoons light brown sugar
½ teaspoon crushed red pepper
1½ teaspoons canola or other vegetable oil
4 skinless, boneless chicken breast halves (about 1½ pounds), cut into 1½-inch cubes
¾ pound fresh spinach, stemmed
1 cup fresh bean sprouts
½ teaspoon grated lime zest
3 tablespoons grated unsweetened coconut

1. In a small bowl, whisk together all but 2 tablespoons of the chicken stock, the lime juice, cornstarch mixture, brown sugar, and red pepper. Set aside.

2. In a wok, heat the oil. Add the chicken cubes and stir-fry over high heat for about 4 minutes, or until done through. Remove with a slotted spoon to a bowl and cover with foil to keep warm.

3. Add the reserved 2 tablespoons of stock to the wok. Add the spinach and stir-fry over medium heat for 30 seconds, until wilted. Transfer to a platter, make a bed of spinach, and keep warm.

4. Increase the heat to medium-high, add the bean sprouts, and stir-fry for 30 seconds. Add the chicken stock mixture and the chicken cubes, and stir-fry for 1 minute more, or until heated through. With a slotted spoon, remove the chicken and bean sprouts from the wok and place over the spinach.

5. Add the lime zest and coconut to the wok, bring to a boil, and cook until the sauce thickens. Pour over the chicken and spinach and serve hot.

Serves 2 to 4

Nutritional Breakdown: *525 calories, 11.2 g fat—19% calories from fat, 197 mg cholesterol, 6.4 g fiber, 1,327 mg sodium*

Pump up the Flavor with Flavor-Infused Oils

Cooking successful low-fat stir-fry dishes requires some planning. One way to hike up the flavor is to infuse oils with various flavors. Use light sesame oil, canola oil, or even olive oil. Use small bottles or jars and add one flavor to each: basil, curry, cinnamon stick, garlic cloves, ginger (if fresh, the oil will need refrigeration), red hot chile, thyme, sage, and so on. For more instructions, see page 12.

CHICKEN-VEGETABLE STIR-FRY

2 tablespoons reduced-sodium soy sauce or tamari
2 tablespoons dry sherry
1 tablespoon rice wine vinegar
2 teaspoons sugar
2 teaspoons cornstarch, dissolved in 1 tablespoon cold water
1 tablespoon fresh lemon juice
¾ pound skinless, boneless chicken breast halves, cut into ½-inch strips
2 cups broccoli florets
2 medium carrots, peeled and sliced on the diagonal
1 green bell pepper, trimmed, seeded, and chopped in 1-inch pieces
2 tablespoons light sesame oil
1 tablespoon minced garlic
1 tablespoon finely minced peeled ginger
1 cup thinly sliced green onion, white and green parts
1 teaspoon dark sesame oil
2 cups cooked white rice

1. In a small bowl, whisk together the soy sauce, sherry, vinegar, and sugar.

2. In a medium mixing bowl, whisk together the cornstarch mixture and lemon juice. Add the chicken strips, stir to coat, and set aside for 15 minutes.

3. Fill a large bowl with ice water and keep near the stove. In a large pot of lightly salted boiling water, blanch the broccoli florets for 1 minute. Remove with a slotted spoon and plunge into the ice water to stop the cooking process. Remove with a slotted spoon and set aside to drain. Repeat with the carrot slices and bell pepper pieces, blanching them separately for 1 minute each.

4. In a wok, heat 1 tablespoon of the light sesame oil over medium-high heat. Add the garlic and ginger and stir-fry for 30 seconds.

5. Add the green onion and stir-fry for 1 minute more. Add the dark sesame oil and, when hot, add the rice and stir-fry for 2 minutes, just to heat the rice through and combine the ingredients. Transfer to a bowl and keep warm.

6. Drain the chicken pieces, reserving the marinade.

7. In the wok, heat the remaining 1 tablespoon light sesame oil. Add the chicken strips and stir-fry for 4 minutes, or until the chicken turns white. Add the reserved marinade, broccoli, carrots, and bell pepper and stir-fry 2 to 3 minutes, or until the vegetables are crisp-tender, the chicken breast pieces are done, and the sauce is thickened. Serve in a bowl with the rice on the side.

Serves 4

Nutritional Breakdown: *368 calories, 9.6 g fat—24% calories from fat, 49.3 mg cholesterol, 3.8 g fiber, 505 mg sodium*

STIR-FRIED CHICKEN WITH CABBAGE AND WATER CHESTNUTS

⅓ cup light teriyaki sauce
1 teaspoon cornstarch, dissolved in 1 tablespoon reduced-sodium soy sauce or tamari
4 skinless, boneless chicken breast halves (about 1½ pounds), cut into 1-inch strips or chunks
1 teaspoon dark sesame oil
2 teaspoons light sesame oil
1 garlic clove, minced
¾ cup thinly sliced water chestnuts
1–2 tablespoons Defatted Chicken Stock (see page 18)
1½ cups shredded napa cabbage

1. In a small bowl, whisk together 1 tablespoon of the teriyaki sauce and the cornstarch mixture. Coat the chicken breast pieces well and set aside for 20 minutes.

2. In a wok, heat both sesame oils. Add the chicken and stir-fry for 3 to 4 minutes, or until done. Remove the chicken with a slotted spoon and set aside.

3. Add the garlic to the hot wok and stir-fry for 30 seconds. Add the water chestnuts and stir-fry for 1 minute more. Add the remaining teriyaki sauce and 1 or 2 tablespoons of chicken stock. Add the cabbage and stir-fry for 1 minute, or until it begins to wilt.

4. Return the chicken pieces to the wok, and stir-fry for 1 minute more, or until the sauce is thickened.

Serves 4

Nutritional Breakdown: *271 calories, 5.6 g fat—19% calories from fat, 98.6 mg cholesterol, 1.2 g fiber, 1,526 mg sodium*

6/3/04 good!

SWEET AND SOUR CHICKEN STIR-FRY

1 tablespoon light sesame oil
1 pound skinless, boneless chicken breast halves, cut into 1-inch strips
1 garlic clove, minced
2 tablespoons dark brown sugar
1½ cups crushed fresh pineapple with 2 tablespoons fresh pineapple juice
3 tablespoons white wine vinegar
2 tablespoons sherry
½ teaspoon grated peeled fresh ginger
½ cup chopped green bell pepper
½ cup chopped red bell pepper
½ cup thinly sliced celery
½ cup carrots, peeled and thinly sliced on the diagonal
¼ cup chopped green onion, white and green parts
1 tablespoon reduced-sodium soy sauce or tamari
2 teaspoons cornstarch, dissolved in 2 tablespoons soy sauce

1. In a wok, heat the oil. Add the chicken and garlic and stir-fry until the chicken is browned, about 4 minutes. Remove from the wok and set aside.

2. In a small bowl, combine the sugar, pineapple juice, vinegar, sherry, and ginger and stir until the sugar is dissolved. Set aside.

3. Add both bell peppers, celery, carrots, and green onion to the wok and stir-fry for 1 minute. Add the soy sauce and continue stir-frying for 1 minute more.

4. Add the chicken pieces to the wok and stir in the cornstarch mixture and pineapple. Bring to a boil, stirring constantly, and cook for 2 minutes more, or until the sauce thickens and the chicken is done. Serve immediately.

Serves 4

Nutritional Breakdown: *252 calories, 5.2 g fat—19% calories from fat, 65.7 mg cholesterol, 2 g fiber, 813 mg sodium*

ORANGE CHICKEN AND PEPPERS WITH CURLY NOODLES

The noodles in this dish come packaged in water. They are usually found in Japanese markets or specialty food sections of the supermarket, and there are many brands to choose from . . . all delicious.

3 tablespoons reduced-sodium soy sauce or tamari
½ cup orange juice
1 pound skinless, boneless chicken breast halves, cut into 1-inch pieces
2 tablespoons rice wine vinegar
1 tablespoon honey
2 teaspoons cornstarch, dissolved in 1 tablespoon cold water
½ teaspoon freshly ground black pepper
2 teaspoons light sesame oil
2–3 cups 1-inch pieces red and yellow bell peppers
1 navel orange, peeled, white pith removed and sections cut from membranes
1 package (8-ounces) fresh Oriental curly noodles, cooked according to package directions, drained, and rinsed

1. In a medium mixing bowl, combine 2 tablespoons of the soy sauce and 1 tablespoon of the orange juice. Add the chicken and stir to coat well. Set aside.
2. In a jar with a tight-fitting lid, combine the remaining soy sauce and orange juice, the vinegar, honey, cornstarch mixture, and pepper and shake to mix well. Set aside.
3. In a wok, heat the oil. Add the chicken pieces and stir-fry over high heat until browned, about 3 to 4 minutes. Transfer to a bowl and set aside.
4. Add the bell peppers to the wok and stir-fry for 2 minutes, or until partially cooked. Return the chicken pieces to the wok along with the reserved orange juice sauce mixture. Bring to a simmer and cook until the chicken pieces are done throughout, about 2 to 3 minutes. In the last 30 seconds of cooking, add the orange sections and noodles, heat through, and serve in 4 soup bowls.

Serves 4

Nutritional Breakdown: *260 calories, 4.3 g fat—15% calories from fat, 74.6 mg cholesterol, 2.7 g fiber, 1,019 mg sodium*

CHICKEN AND ASPARAGUS STIR-FRY

2 teaspoons cornstarch, dissolved in 1 tablespoon chicken stock
1 teaspoon coarse salt
4 skinless, boneless chicken breast halves (about 1½ pounds), cut into 1½-inch cubes
2 tablespoons light sesame oil
2 tablespoons minced onion
2 garlic cloves, minced
2 tablespoons minced parsley
¼ teaspoon crushed red pepper
2 cups 1½-inch pieces asparagus tips
½ teaspoon salt
1 tablespoon fresh orange juice
1 teaspoon grated orange zest
Freshly ground black pepper

1. In a medium bowl, combine the cornstarch mixture, coarse salt, and chicken cubes and toss to mix well. Marinate, refrigerated, for 1 hour. Drain the chicken well before cooking.
2. In a wok, heat 1 tablespoon of the oil. Add the chicken and stir-fry until browned and done, about 4 to 5 minutes. Remove to a bowl and set aside.
3. In the wok, heat the remaining 1 tablespoon oil. Add the onion and garlic and stir-fry for 15 seconds. Add 1 tablespoon of the parsley and the red pepper and stir-fry for 10 seconds more. Add the asparagus tips, ½ teaspoon salt, orange juice, and zest and cook to crisp-tender, about 2 minutes.
4. Return the chicken pieces to the wok and stir-fry just to heat through, about 1 minute more. Season with black pepper to taste. Toss with the remaining 1 tablespoon parsley, and serve immediately.

Serves 4

Nutritional Breakdown: *280 calories, 9.14 g fat—30% calories from fat, 98.6 mg cholesterol, 1.6 g fiber, 939 mg sodium*

Stir-Fry Sweets

The wok is a perfect place to make a stir-fry dessert. Cube a variety of fruits and toss, using a small amount of cinnamon and unsalted butter. You can serve the fruit rolled in a crepe made with orange juice instead of water in the batter. This makes a good dessert with any low-fat chicken breast dish.

CHICKEN AND MELON STIR-FRY

1 teaspoon dark sesame oil
2 teaspoons reduced-sodium soy sauce or tamari
1 tablespoon dry white wine
1 teaspoon oyster sauce
½ teaspoon ground ginger
2 teaspoons cornstarch, dissolved in 1 tablespoon water
½ teaspoon sugar
Pinch of salt
Pinch of freshly ground black pepper
1 pound skinless, boneless chicken breast halves, cut into 1-inch-thick slices
1 tablespoon peanut oil
2 teaspoons minced garlic
½ cup snow peas, cut in half on the diagonal
4 green onions, cut into 1-inch pieces, white and green parts, divided
½ medium cantaloupe, cut into balls using a melon baller
½ medium-firm honeydew melon, cut into balls using a melon baller
2 tablespoons toasted sesame seeds for garnish

1. In a small bowl, combine the dark sesame oil, soy sauce, white wine, oyster sauce, ginger, cornstarch mixture, sugar, salt, pepper, and chicken slices. Toss to mix well and marinate for 1 hour.

2. In a wok, heat half of the peanut oil. Add the garlic and stir-fry over medium-high heat for 30 seconds. Add the snow peas and the green onions and stir-fry for 30 seconds more. Add the cantaloupe and honeydew melon balls and gently stir-fry just until heated through, about 1 minute. Remove all the ingredients to a bowl with a slotted spoon. Set aside.

3. Drain the chicken and reserve the marinade. Add the remaining peanut oil to the wok. Add the chicken and stir-fry until the chicken is done throughout, about 4 minutes. Return the melon balls and snow peas to the wok and stir to combine. Drizzle in the marinade along the side of the wok and stir-fry for 1 minute more, until the sauce has thickened. Serve on a platter and garnish with the sesame seeds.

Serves 4 to 6

Nutritional Breakdown: *270 calories, 8.5 g fat—28% calories from fat, 65.7 mg cholesterol, 2.3 g fiber, 283 mg sodium*

CHICKEN AND SNOW PEA RICE SALAD

This chicken breast and fresh snow pea stir-fry is prepared and cooled before serving over lettuce leaves. It makes a wonderful appetizer.

4 skinless, boneless chicken breast halves (about 1½ pounds), cut into ¼-inch strips
1 teaspoon cornstarch, dissolved in 1 tablespoon dry sherry
1 teaspoon reduced-sodium soy sauce or tamari
½ teaspoon crushed red pepper
1 tablespoon light sesame oil
½ large onion, sliced paper thin
1 teaspoon minced fresh peeled ginger
2 garlic cloves, minced
1½ pounds snow peas, trimmed
¾ cup chopped green onion, white and green parts, plus 2 tablespoons finely chopped for garnish
2 tablespoons rice wine vinegar
3 tablespoons fresh lemon juice
2 teaspoons sherry
1 teaspoon honey
Salt and freshly ground white pepper
3 cups freshly cooked white rice
2 tablespoons toasted sesame seeds
3 tablespoons chopped flat-leaf parsley
4 cups mixed salad greens of choice

1. In a small bowl, combine the chicken strips, cornstarch mixture, soy sauce, and the red pepper. Mix well and marinate for 10 minutes.

2. In a wok, heat half of the oil. Add the onion and stir-fry for 1 minute. Add the ginger and garlic and stir-fry for 30 seconds more. Add the chicken strips and the marinade and stir-fry for 2 to 3 minutes more, or until the strips are done. Remove the contents of the wok to a bowl and set aside.

3. In the wok, heat the remaining oil. Add the pea pods and the ¾ cup of green onion and stir-fry for 1 minute. Add the vinegar, 1 tablespoon of the lemon juice, the sherry, and honey and stir-fry for 1 minute more. Add the chicken mixture to the wok, season with salt and pepper, and stir-fry for 1 to 2 minutes more, or just until the chicken strips are warmed through. Transfer the mixture to a bowl and cool to room temperature.

4. In a large mixing bowl, toss together the chicken and pea mixture, rice, the remaining 2 tablespoons of lemon juice, the sesame seeds, and parsley. Serve on the salad greens and sprinkle with the remaining green onion.

Serves 4 to 6

Nutritional Breakdown: *557 calories, 8.8 g fat—15% calories from fat, 98.6 mg cholesterol, 7.5 g fiber, 212 mg sodium*

Nonstick Wok vs. Traditional

Both are good for low-fat cooking. Both have their own advantages. If you're using a nonstick surface, remember to keep the heat to medium, and to add the fat before heating; never add fat to a heated nonstick pan. Traditional wok surfaces cook the food faster, since they can be heated to higher temperatures; however, they require a little oil to prevent sticking. Plan to have a variety of wood and/or metal cooking utensils available as required for the various cooking surfaces.

Note: The stir-fry recipes in this chapter are written for traditional wok surfaces, using high temperatures to stir-fry ingredients. For nonstick wok (or skillet) surfaces, adjust the temperature to medium and increase the cooking time appropriately.

Get Ready, Get Set, Stir-Fry

Start your stir-fry by lining up all the ingredients in order of use, including marinated chicken breast pieces, uniformly chopped vegetables, and chopped fresh herbs, as well as the sauce ingredients that go in last. Keep proper utensils at arm's length, including a cover for the wok and cooking tools for stir-frying as well as for removing the food from the wok. It's also a good idea to have the table set and ready to go. Ask your family or friends to gather round the table when the ingredients start to sizzle in the hot wok. Remember, don't overfill the wok; if you do, there won't be enough surface to cook the foods evenly. Divide the total amount of ingredients into several batches if necessary, keeping the already-cooked ingredients warm under foil until all is ready to be served.

Steam

Fresh! It's an appropriate thought for any food cooked in a steamer. The finished food keeps its shape and color more readily than with other cooking processes. But when you consider the facts, steaming is no more than a delicate, though superhot, vapor that cooks foods very quickly. It's also totally fat free! The first step in creating a successful "steamed" chicken breast recipe is giving the vapor some character. Before placing the steamer basket over the hot water in the wok or stockpot, consider adding some of these flavorful ingredients: whole and toasted ground spices, citrus peel, stock, wine or sake, fresh herbs, and aromatics (see pages 113 and 116 for complete steaming instructions). First boil these ingredients for 5 minutes to allow the flavors to infuse the water. Then, during this easy and healthful cooking process, a transfer of subtle flavors will naturally take place between the vapor and the chicken breast. Each of the following steaming recipes calls for a customized steaming broth. For entertaining, try the delicate Stuffed Chicken Rolls and Yellow Pepper Sauce (page 114), or Steamed Lemon Chicken Breast Bundles (page 107), in which lettuce leaves are used as natural wrappings. And, for the basis of a light shredded salad, use Soy and Lime Chicken Breasts Steamed in Sake (page 116). It's also possible to cook several dishes at once in a two- or three-tiered steamer. This has got to be the best use for hot air since ballooning.

STEAMED LEMON CHICKEN BREAST BUNDLES

An Oriental two-tiered bamboo steamer is called for in this recipe. See page 113 for steaming details.

Steaming Broth

6 to 8 garlic cloves, smashed
2 lemons, cut into thin, round slices
Fresh thyme sprig
1 teaspoon black peppercorns
4 cups spring water, or more
½ cup white wine

Lemon Chicken Breast

12 large romaine lettuce leaves
12 long strips green onion, green part only
2 skinless, boneless chicken breast halves (about ¾ pound)
2 teaspoons grated lemon zest
1 cup cooked white rice
1 medium yellow bell pepper, seeded and finely diced
2 tablespoons finely chopped green onion, white and green parts
¼ cup chopped flat-leaf parsley
2 garlic cloves, minced
2 teaspoons fresh lemon juice
2 teaspoons coarse salt
½ teaspoon freshly ground white pepper

1. Place the smashed garlic, lemon slices, thyme sprig, peppercorns, spring water, and wine in a wok. Bring to a boil, cover, lower the heat, and simmer for 20 minutes.
2. Meanwhile, place the lettuce leaves and green onion strips in the top tier of a steamer and cover tightly. Place the steamer over the top of the simmering broth and steam until the lettuce leaves are wilted, about 30 seconds. Turn the heat off. Transfer the vegetables from the steamer to a work surface. Reserve the broth in the wok.
3. Reserve the green onion strips. Lay the lettuce leaves flat. Trim down the tough ends and the heavy center stems.
4. In the bowl of a food processor fitted with a metal blade, process the chicken until a spreadlike consistency forms. Add the lemon zest and pulse.
5. Transfer to a medium mixing bowl and stir in the rice, bell pepper, chopped green onion, parsley, minced garlic, lemon juice, salt, and pepper.
6. Divide the chicken mixture into 12 equal mounds. Place a mound in the center of each lettuce leaf. Fold the

sides in toward the center and then fold the bottom up and over the filling. Finally, fold down the top portion of each leaf to cover the filling completely. Tie each bundle with one of the steamed green onion strips. Repeat until all the bundles are filled and tied.

7. Position the bundles in the steamer so that they are just touching. Do not crowd or press together.

8. Bring the broth in the wok to a boil over high heat, reduce to a simmer, and place the steamer on top. Steam the bundles for 15 to 17 minutes, or until done. The bundles should be moist, tender, and cooked throughout.

Serves 4

Nutritional Breakdown: *246 calories, 1.7 g fat—7% calories from fat, 49.3 mg cholesterol, 5 g fiber, 1,148 mg sodium*

What Exactly Is a Steamer?

A steamer consists of a vessel to hold and boil the water. Fitting precisely on top of that is a steaming basket containing one, two, and sometimes even three tiers. All the recipes in this chapter have been tested by steaming in the second tier up from the water in a traditional Asian bamboo steamer, which is usually the easiest way to cook. The top must have a very tight lid to hold in the steam until the food is done. Many devices made for steaming work very well, including Asian bamboo steamers, collapsible vegetable steaming baskets and bamboo inserts used in saucepans, woks, and skillets with lids; inserts that fit on top of saucepans, and those that are lowered into the pan but are totally detached; pasta cooking pots with inserts; and a variety of pans that have racks that are lowered into the pan, most of which are used in the oven rather than on top of the stove, although there is no law against oven steaming.

STEAMED CHICKEN BREAST AND ZUCCHINI BUNDLES

Vapor infused with the essence of fresh rosemary and white wine cooks these bundles, adding subtle flavors that complement and enhance the delicate low-fat filling. Experiment by creating a steaming broth that reflects your own favorite flavors. Almost any strong-flavored ingredients will work well.

Steaming Broth

1 cup white wine
2 cups spring water, or more
1 lemon, cut in thin, round slices
3 branches fresh rosemary
1 teaspoon black peppercorns

Chicken Breast

1 pound small zucchini
1 tablespoon coarse salt
½ cup minced flat-leaf parsley
1 teaspoon minced garlic
1½ teaspoons grated lemon zest
Salt and freshly ground white pepper
¾ pound skinless, boneless chicken breast halves, cut into small pieces
1 large egg white
2 tablespoons minced shallot
12 large romaine lettuce leaves
12 long strips of green onion, green part only
Lemon wedges for garnish

1. Place the wine, water, lemon slices, rosemary branches, and peppercorns in a wok. Bring to a boil, cover, lower the heat, and simmer for 20 minutes. Reserve the broth in the wok.
2. Meanwhile, soak the zucchini in a bowl of cold water with the coarse salt for 30 minutes to remove the bitterness. Rinse and then pat dry with paper towels. Coarsely grate the zucchini with a hand grater. Set in a strainer to continue draining for a few minutes more.
3. In a medium bowl, combine the parsley, garlic, lemon zest, and zucchini. Season lightly with salt and pepper and set aside.
4. In the bowl of a food processor fitted with the metal blade, process the chicken for about 20 seconds. Add the egg white and process to a smooth consistency. Add the shallots and pulse just to mix.
5. Transfer the chicken mixture to the bowl with the zucchini mixture. Adjust the seasoning with salt and pepper. Set aside.

6. Heat the broth in the wok to a simmer. Place the lettuce leaves and green onion strips in the top tier of a steamer and cover tightly. Place the steamer over the simmering broth and steam until the lettuce leaves and the green onion strips are wilted, about 30 seconds. Turn the heat off. Transfer the vegetables to a work surface.Reserve the broth in the wok.

7. Lay the lettuce leaves flat. Trim down the tough end and the heavy center stems.

8. Divide the chicken mixture into 12 equal mounds. Place a mound in the center of each lettuce leaf. Fold the sides in toward the center and then fold the bottom up and over the filling. Finally, fold down the top portion of each leaf to cover the filling completely. Tie each bundle with one of the steamed green onion strips. Repeat until all the bundles are filled and tied.

9. Position the bundles in the steamer so that they are just touching. Do not crowd or press together.

10. Bring the broth in the wok to a boil over high heat, reduce to a simmer, and place the steamer on top. Steam the bundles for 15 to 17 minutes, or until done. The bundles should be moist, tender, and cooked through. Arrange the bundles on a platter and garnish with the lemon wedges.

Serves 4 as a main course, or 6 to 8 as an appetizer

Nutritional Breakdown: *196 calories, 1.7 g fat—8% calories from fat, 49.3 mg cholesterol, 5 g fiber, 1,697 mg sodium*

Where to Get a Steamer If Your Local Gourmet Cookware Store Is Still Waiting for Its Shipment from Hong Kong

Try trusty sources like Williams-Sonoma at 1-800-541-2233. Or, if you're lucky enough to have an area in your city designated as "Chinatown," as we do in Los Angeles, then you will only need to visit the Asian market to find an amazing array of bamboo steamers. On my last trip, I found them sized from 9 inches to about 36 inches across. Some even had carved cedarwood bottoms, so that the vapor would pick up the flavor of the wood and transport it to the ingredients above. Steamers are priced as low as $13. While you're there, have lunch, and ask for steamed anything, just to try the real thing before your experiments begin. If you want a metal pot with a fitted steaming basket, try the cookware section of any department store.

CHICKEN AND PORTOBELLO MUSHROOM SALAD

This salad is served warm, which makes it a perfect winter or fall dish.

4 skinless, boneless chicken breast halves (about 1½ pounds)
1 teaspoon dried basil
Salt and freshly ground black pepper
4 teaspoons fresh lemon juice
2 tablespoons extra-virgin olive oil
2 large portobello mushrooms, stemmed and chopped in large chunks
2 tablespoons finely chopped flat-leaf parsley
2 large garlic cloves, crushed
4 sun-dried tomato halves, softened in hot water for 15 minutes, drained
¼ cup peeled, seeded, and chopped plum tomatoes
2 tablespoons red wine vinegar
4 cups mixed baby lettuce or salad greens of choice

1. To steam the chicken breasts, place each breast in a separate piece of heavy-duty plastic wrap or foil large enough to enclose the breast. Sprinkle on the basil, salt, pepper, and lemon juice. Tightly wrap the plastic or foil around the chicken breasts.

2. In a wok, bring water to a boil. Place a bamboo steamer on top of the water and lower the heat to a simmer. Place the wrapped chicken breasts in the steamer, in the second tier up from the water. Cover and steam for 15 to 17 minutes, or until done through. Remove the packages from the steamer and open. Cool the breasts in their juices, and reserve.

3. Meanwhile, in a large nonstick skillet or sauté pan, heat 1 tablespoon of the oil. Add the portobello chunks and cook, stirring occasionally, until the liquid from the mushrooms has almost evaporated, about 4 minutes. Add the parsley and ⅓ cup of the reserved juice from steaming the chicken. Season with salt and pepper and continue cooking, over moderately high heat, until the liquid has evaporated, about 5 minutes more. Transfer the mushrooms to a plate and let cool to room temperature.

4. To make the vinaigrette, in a blender, place the garlic, softened sun-dried tomatoes, chopped plum tomatoes, vinegar, and a pinch of salt and pepper and blend to a smooth consistency. With the motor running, add the remaining 1 tablespoon of oil in a thin but steady stream.

5. Place the salad greens on 4 large salad plates. Thinly slice the chicken breasts on the diagonal and arrange over the greens.

6. Toss the mushroom pieces in the vinaigrette and scatter over the chicken and greens. Pass the pepper mill.

Serves 4

Nutritional Breakdown: *263 calories, 7.6 g fat—26% calories from fat, 98.6 mg cholesterol, 1.7 g fiber, 155 mg sodium*

CHICKEN BREASTS WITH CHINESE BLACK BEAN PUREE

This dish brings with it a full-flavored combination of ingredients often found in Chinese dishes, namely, ginger, soy, oyster sauce, and fermented black beans.

2 teaspoons cornstarch, dissolved in 2 tablespoons medium-dry sherry
1 tablespoon peanut oil
¼ cup minced fermented black beans (available in Asian markets and some supermarkets)
1 tablespoon minced fresh peeled ginger
1 tablespoon minced garlic
⅔ cup Defatted Chicken Stock (see page 18)
1 tablespoon oyster sauce
1 tablespoon reduced-sodium soy sauce or tamari
4 skinless, boneless chicken breast halves (about 1½ pounds)
1 tablespoon medium-dry sherry
1 tablespoon dark sesame oil
¼ cup chopped green onion, plus 2 tablespoons for garnish

1. Place the cornstarch mixture in a small saucepan. Set aside.

2. In a wok, heat the peanut oil over medium-high heat. Add the black beans, ginger, and garlic and stir-fry for 15 seconds. Add the chicken stock, oyster sauce, and soy sauce, bring to a boil, and cook for 2 minutes. Transfer to the bowl of a mini food processor and process until smooth. Place in the saucepan with the cornstarch mixture and cook, stirring constantly, over medium heat until the sauce thickens, about 1 minute. Remove from the heat and set the pan aside.

3. Wipe the wok clean and bring water to a boil for steaming. Position a bamboo steamer on top of the wok.

4. Place the chicken breasts in a heatproof dish that fits loosely inside the bamboo steamer. Sprinkle with the sherry, sesame oil, and ¼ cup of the chopped green onion. Place the dish in the steamer, in the second tier up from the water. Steam for 12 to 17 minutes, or until done throughout. Do not overcook.

5. Meanwhile, reheat the black bean sauce. Place the breasts in 4 individual shallow bowls. Stir any juices remaining in the steaming dish into the sauce and heat through. Pour the sauce over the chicken breasts, and sprinkle on the remaining 2 tablespoons green onion.

Serves 4

Nutritional Breakdown: *306 calories, 9.4 g fat—30% calories from fat, 99 mg cholesterol, 1.1 g fiber, 718 mg sodium*

Steamer Timings Vary from Bamboo to Metal, and Even from Shape to Shape

This means a little more testing will be necessary. If the seal is not perfectly tight, which is often the case with bamboo, the cooking time can be as much as 50 percent more than with the top-of-the-line precision heavy-gauge stainless steel steamers. Cooking in stackable steamers, no matter what they're made of, takes a little longer in general. Use the steamer guide to follow as a starting point, prepare one chicken breast in your steamer, and then adjust the timings that work best for you by adding or subtracting time in one-minute segments.

Timings in Minutes for 6- to 8-Ounce breasts:

Bamboo stackable steamer: 12–17
Stainless steel steamer: 12–14

STUFFED CHICKEN ROLLS AND YELLOW PEPPER SAUCE

This is basically chicken breast stuffed with a light mousselike chicken breast mixture. It is a very delicate dish. This sauce recipe can be used to make zucchini, onion, or other vegetable purees.

Chicken Rolls

2 large whole skinless, boneless chicken breasts, pounded between plastic wrap to ¼ inch thick
Salt and freshly ground white pepper
¾ pound ground skinless, boneless chicken breast meat
1 large egg white
1 garlic clove, minced
2 shallots, minced
2 tablespoons mixed fresh chopped herbs (such as oregano, chervil, sage, tarragon, and basil)
3 tablespoons snipped fresh chives
1 cup finely chopped spinach

Sauce

2 teaspoons unsalted butter
2 large yellow bell peppers, seeded and cut into pieces
1 garlic clove, crushed
1 tablespoon chopped shallots
2 sprigs fresh thyme
3 cups Rich Chicken Stock (see page 16)
Salt and freshly ground white pepper

1. On a flat work surface, place each whole chicken breast on a large double layer of plastic wrap. Season with a small amount of salt and pepper.

2. In a medium mixing bowl, stir together the ground chicken, egg white, garlic, shallots, herbs, chives, and spinach.

3. Spread half the chicken mixture over each whole chicken breast, leaving a 1-inch border free of the mixture. Starting with the long end, roll up the chicken breasts like a jelly roll. Wrap the chicken rolls tightly in the plastic wrap, seam side down. Place in a heatproof dish that fits loosely in a bamboo steamer.

4. In a wok, bring water to a simmer. Position a steamer on top of the wok. Place the dish in the steamer in the second tier up from the water. Cover tightly and steam the chicken sausage for about 12 to 17 minutes, or until done throughout. Remove the dish from the steamer, transfer the chicken rolls to a work surface, and let cool at least 10 minutes. Slice in rounds.

5. While the chicken is cooking, make the sauce. In a medium nonstick sauté pan or skillet, melt the butter. Add the bell peppers, garlic, shallots, and thyme and sauté the vegetables over medium heat for about 2 minutes. Add the chicken stock and simmer, uncovered, for about 20 minutes. Remove the thyme sprigs, transfer the mixture to a blender, and blend until smooth. Season with salt and pepper.

6. Serve slices of the chicken rolls with the sauce.

Serves 4, or 6 to 8 as an appetizer

Nutritional Breakdown: *219 calories, 6.3 g fat—26% calories from fat, 67.9 mg cholesterol, 2.8 g fiber, 902 mg sodium*

More "Steamed" Chicken Breast Recipes Are Hiding in This Book

Several other recipes in this book can be converted easily into steaming recipes. Wrap the chicken breasts and other ingredients in aluminum foil, parchment, or heavy-duty cooking plastic wrap before steaming.

- Baked Chicken-Stuffed Zucchini (page 57)
- Chicken, Rice, and Spinach Filled Cabbage Rolls (page 56)
- Glazed Chicken Loaf (page 61)
- Balsamic Chicken Breasts with Vegetables en Papillote (page 67)
- Tarragon Chicken Breasts with Artichokes (page 72)

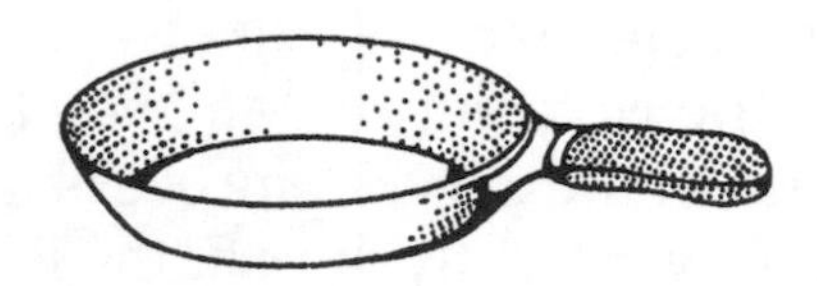

SOY AND LIME CHICKEN BREASTS STEAMED IN SAKE

4 skinless, boneless chicken breast halves (about 1½ pounds)
2¼ cups sake (Japanese rice wine)
⅓ cup reduced-sodium soy sauce
2 teaspoons grated lime zest
¼ cup fresh lime juice
2 garlic cloves, minced
1 tablespoon hot Oriental mustard
1 tablespoon peanut oil
¼ cup finely chopped green onion, white and green parts
½ teaspoon freshly ground white pepper
Lime zest, cut into very thin strips for garnish

1. Place the chicken breasts in a heatproof dish that fits loosely inside a bamboo steamer.
2. To a wok, add 2 cups of the sake and enough water to fill just below the bottom of the steamer. Bring to a simmer.
3. Position the steamer on the wok and place the dish in the steamer in the second tier up from the water. Cover tightly and steam the chicken until done throughout, about 12 to 17 minutes.
4. Meanwhile, in a small bowl, whisk together the soy sauce, grated lime zest, lime juice, garlic, and mustard. In a thin but steady stream, add the oil, whisking constantly until well combined. Stir in the green onion and pepper.
5. In a small saucepan, boil the remaining ¼ cup sake over medium-high heat and reduce to 1 tablespoon, about 5 minutes. Stir in the soy-and-lime mixture and heat through. Drizzle over the chicken, turning to coat well. Garnish with the strips of lime zest.

Serves 4

Nutritional Breakdown: *270 calories, 5.7 g fat—19% calories from fat, 98.6 mg cholesterol, 0.6 g fiber, 1,518 mg sodium*

Don't Take the Lid Off, Please

. . . until you think the chicken is completely done. Hot steam will burn you, and you'll interfere with the steaming process. Always turn the heat off first. Lift the lid of the steamer away from you, so that the steam escapes out the back. Remember, if you let the steam out while cooking and then replace the lid, the results will resemble poached, not steamed, chicken.

CHICKEN BREASTS WITH FRUIT SALSA

4 skinless, boneless chicken breast halves (about 1½ pounds)
Salt and freshly ground black pepper
Juice of 1 lemon
2 green onions, coarsely chopped

Salsa

2 cups peeled and diced peaches
2 cups diced banana
½ cup finely chopped red onion
2 tablespoons finely chopped fresh cilantro, plus 1 tablespoon for garnish
1 small jalapeño pepper, stemmed, seeded, and minced
1 small garlic clove, minced
2 tablespoons Champagne or white wine vinegar
2 tablespoons fresh lime juice

1. Place the chicken breasts in a heat-proof dish that loosely fits in a bamboo steamer. Season the chicken with salt and pepper.

2. To a wok, add just enough water to reach nearly to the bottom of the steamer, the lemon juice, and green onions and bring to a simmer.

3. Position the steamer on top of the wok. Put the dish in the steamer in the second tier up from the liquid. Cover tightly and steam the chicken until done throughout, about 12 to 17 minutes. Cool to room temperature.

4. Meanwhile, combine the peaches, banana, onion, 2 tablespoons of the cilantro, the jalapeño, garlic, vinegar, and lime juice. Toss to mix and marinate for 30 minutes before serving.

5. Thinly slice the chicken on the diagonal, arrange on 4 individual plates, sprinkle with the remaining 1 tablespoon cilantro, and serve with the fruit salsa.

Serves 4

Nutritional Breakdown: *318 calories, 2.6 g fat—8% calories from fat, 98.6 mg cholesterol, 3.8 g fiber, 178 mg sodium*

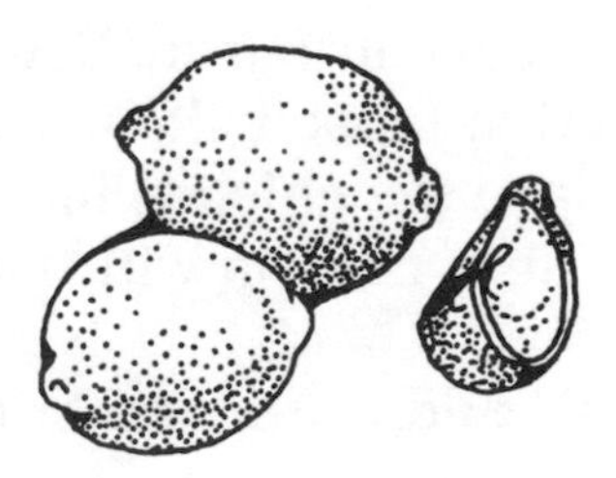

PEANUT AND SESAME CHICKEN SALAD

¼ cup sake or dry white wine
4 skinless, boneless chicken breast halves (about 1½ pounds), pounded between plastic wrap to flatten slightly
Salt and freshly ground white pepper
2 tablespoons chicken stock
1 tablespoon tahini (sesame paste)
1 tablespoon natural smooth peanut butter (avoid the oil that collects on the top of the peanut butter)
2 tablespoons rice wine vinegar
1 tablespoon reduced-sodium soy sauce or tamari
1 teaspoon fresh lemon juice
½ teaspoon honey
1 large head Romaine lettuce, tough outer leaves removed and cut into chiffonade
¼ cup finely chopped green onion, green part only
2 tablespoons toasted sesame seeds

1. Pour the sake into a shallow heat-proof dish that loosely fits in a bamboo steamer. Place the chicken into the bottom of the dish. Season with salt and pepper.
2. To a wok, add water and bring to a simmer.
3. Position the steamer on top of the wok. Place the dish in the steamer, the second tier up from the water. Cover tightly and steam the chicken for about 12 to 17 minutes, or until done throughout. Remove the dish from the steamer and let the chicken cool for 10 minutes in the sake. Combine the chicken stock with 2 tablespoons of the steaming liquid and set aside. Slice the chicken on the diagonal into thin slices or chunks. Chill thoroughly before tossing with the dressing.
4. Meanwhile, to make the dressing, in a glass jar with a tight-fitting lid, combine the tahini, peanut butter, vinegar, reserved stock mixture, soy sauce, lemon juice, and honey and shake to mix well. Drizzle the dressing over the chicken. Serve the chicken on a mound of the romaine lettuce, sprinkled with the green onions and toasted sesame seeds.

Serves 4

Nutritional Breakdown: *301 calories, 8.9 g fat—28% calories from fat, 98.6 mg cholesterol, 2.9 g fiber, 351 mg sodium*

Grill, Broil & Smoke

These days, with low-fat cooking at the forefront of the food scene, the broiler is making a comeback. This modern-day, all-weather, reliable, fast, and fat-free cooking machine couldn't be more ready when you are. Although, with a choice between broiling or grilling out in the backyard, with friends and neighbors relaxing and getting ready for a feast, the broiler usually ends up cold until bad weather arrives.

Chicken breasts cooked on the grill just can't be beat. And are they low fat? Naturally! This lean white meat is especially flavorful when allowed to sit for a while to soak up the essences in a complex marinade. (See page 129 for lots of good ones.) Even a basting barbecue sauce can transform the chicken breast into a flavor-packed entrée.

Once you've chosen a cooking method, whether it's grilling, broiling, or smoking, the real fun begins. Use the cooked breasts in any number of dishes, such as gazpacho and pasta; or alongside garlic-mashed potatoes; in salads; on couscous; and even between a bun, inside a tortilla, or with papaya-mango salsa on the side.

In addition, for those who want to start smoking foods, this is the place. And there are lots of easy tips to get you going. The only problem is deciding which recipe to try first.

FUSILLI WITH CHICKEN, HERBS, AND OVEN-DRIED TOMATOES

Any type of corkscrew or tubular pasta can be substituted, or try spinach, tomato, or other vegetable-based pastas to make this dish even more visually appealing. The oven-dried tomatoes, which are a milder homemade version of standard sun-dried tomatoes, are an interesting touch. Grill the chicken breasts in advance, so the dish can be easily tossed together in just minutes.

2 large ripe tomatoes, thinly sliced
½ teaspoon dried basil or oregano
4 skinless, boneless chicken breast halves (about 1½ pounds), pounded between plastic wrap to ½ inch thick
Salt and freshly ground black pepper
1½ tablespoons extra-virgin olive oil
4 garlic cloves, very finely minced
3 shallots, minced
3 medium carrots, peeled and cut into julienne
1 cup Defatted Chicken Stock (see page 18)
¼ cup dry white wine
5 tablespoons mixed chopped fresh herbs (such as parsley, thyme, basil, oregano, and rosemary)
¾ pound dried fusilli or other corkscrew or tubular pasta
1½ teaspoons unsalted butter

1. Preheat the oven to 150° F. Sprinkle the tomatoes with the dried basil or oregano and place in the preheated oven for 2 hours. Cool the tomatoes slightly, and chop.
2. Fire up the grill or heat the broiler. Lightly coat the grill or broiling rack with cooking spray. Season the chicken breasts with salt and pepper and grill or broil until browned on both sides and done throughout, about 3 to 4 minutes per side.
3. Cut the chicken into large julienne strips about ½ inch wide and 1½ inches long. Set aside and keep warm.
4. In a large skillet or sauté pan lightly coated with cooking spray, heat 1 tablespoon of the oil. Cook the garlic and shallots over medium heat until tender. Add the carrots, chopped tomatoes, chicken stock, wine, fresh herbs, and salt and pepper to taste. Lower the heat and cook until the carrots are tender, about 5 minutes.

5. Meanwhile, in a large stockpot filled with lightly salted boiling water, cook the fusilli to al dente. Drain.

6. In a large nonstick skillet, heat the remaining ½ tablespoon oil and the butter. Toss the fusilli and the chicken breast pieces in the butter and oil until well coated and the chicken pieces are heated through. Toss in the vegetables, adjust the seasoning, and serve in large warmed pasta bowls.

Serves 4 to 6

Nutritional Breakdown: *663 calories, 11 g fat—15% calories from fat, 119 mg cholesterol, 4.2 g fiber, 357 mg sodium*

Try It Smoked . . . It's Easier than You Think!

Tending the fires is not necessary with this flavor-enhancing cooking method. Foods are slowly smoked, and flavored, in an enclosed barbecue/ smoker by the direct, although low, heat of the smoldering hardwood charcoal embers—usually left over from grilling. Water-soaked hardwood chips provide the smoke. Once the food to be smoked is in place, just throw on some wood chips, slam down the lid of the smoker, and come back later. Then, finish the chicken breast in the oven for a few minutes before serving. This is low-fat, high-flavor cooking at its best.

Many kinds of foods can be smoked, such as chicken breasts, chicken rolls (see page 114 for recipe), or just about anything that cooks fairly fast (i.e., not whole chickens or turkeys) and that won't disintegrate during smoking and fall into the bottom of the barbecue. Along with chicken breasts, try smoking tomatoes, eggplant, onion halves, squash, portobello mushrooms, or whole heads of garlic to use in an amazingly delicious smoked vegetable ragout or sauce.

GRILLED ROSEMARY CHICKEN, ASPARAGUS, AND RED ONION SALAD

This strongly flavored Stilton vinaigrette requires a surprisingly small amount of cheese to add dimension to the salad.

4 skinless, boneless chicken breast halves (about 1½ pounds)
2 branches fresh rosemary leaves, pounded slightly
3 tablespoons dry white wine or vermouth
2 tablespoons fresh lemon juice
2 teaspoons Dijon mustard
Salt and freshly ground black pepper
1½ pounds thin asparagus, stems trimmed
1 tablespoon extra-virgin olive oil
1 red onion, peeled, quartered, and very thinly sliced
4 medium heads Boston lettuce, leaves separated but left whole

Vinaigrette
2 tablespoons crumbled Stilton or other aged blue cheese (such as Roquefort or Gorgonzola)
1 tablespoon extra-virgin olive oil
1 tablespoon vegetable oil
2 tablespoons Defatted Chicken Stock (see page 18)
2 tablespoons nonfat milk
2 tablespoons Champagne vinegar
½ teaspoon freshly ground black pepper
¼ teaspoon salt, or more

1. Place the chicken breasts in a small shallow dish. Nestle the rosemary branches in between the breasts.
2. Whisk together the wine or vermouth, lemon juice, Dijon mustard, salt, and pepper until well combined. Drizzle half the marinade over the chicken breasts, coating on all sides. Cover the dish tightly with plastic wrap and marinate for 2 hours in the refrigerator. Reserve the remaining marinade.
3. In a sauté pan or high-sided skillet large enough to hold all the asparagus, cook the asparagus in lightly salted boiling water over medium-high heat to crisp-tender, about 3 minutes. Do not overcook. Drain the asparagus and cool under cold running water. Set aside to drain. Cut into bite-size pieces.
4. Fire up the grill or turn the broiler to high. Lightly coat the grilling rack or

broiling pan with cooking spray. Remove the chicken from the marinade, and discard the rosemary and the marinade. Grill or broil the chicken 3 to 4 minutes per side, or until done. Cool slightly before slicing into ¼-inch pieces.

5. In a large nonstick skillet, heat the oil. Cook the onion, stirring frequently, over medium-high heat until browned and crisp, about 5 minutes. Do not burn. Remove from the pan with a slotted spoon or spatula. Place on paper towels to drain off any excess oil.

6. To make the vinaigrette, in a blender or the bowl of a mini food processor, combine the blue cheese, olive and vegetable oils, chicken stock, milk, vinegar, pepper, and salt and process until smooth and well combined.

7. Place the lettuce in a large mixing bowl and drizzle on the vinaigrette. Toss gently. Divide among 4 plates.

8. Place the chicken breast pieces and the asparagus tips in a clean, medium-size mixing bowl, and toss with the reserved marinade. Adjust the seasoning with a pinch of salt. Place the chicken and asparagus on the lettuce. Top with the crispy red onion.

Serves 4 (generous salads)

Nutritional Breakdown: *333 calories, 8.9 g fat—24% calories from fat, 103 mg cholesterol, 6.5 g fiber, 414 mg sodium*

Watt a Grill!

Undoubtedly, backyard grills have always worked overtime on weekends. But where can we take these methods to get the great taste of the grill on a freezing Tuesday evening in the middle of February? Well, lucky for us a bunch of folks out there have come up with some different approaches, and these days, they're grilling everything from papaya to pizzas—and doing it very well. Yes, there are new ways to get that great grill taste (though not necessarily the aroma imparted by fruitwood smoke) anytime, anywhere, as long as there's an electrical outlet nearby. I'm talking about mini indoor grills, which come in a variety of sizes and fit on the countertop. The one used to test some of these recipes is Farberware's The Bistro Grill. It is easy to use and easy to clean, and it looks just right . . . like a little outdoor grill.

SPICY GAZPACHO WITH CHICKEN AND AVOCADO

For more texture and flavor, add crushed, baked tortilla chips to this soup.

12 large plum tomatoes
2 skinless, boneless chicken breast halves, (about ¾ pound), pounded between plastic wrap to ½ inch thick
Salt and freshly ground black pepper
⅓ cup peeled, chopped cucumber
¼ cup chopped red onion
¼ cup chopped celery
¼ cup seeded and chopped red bell pepper
1 large garlic clove, finely minced
2 teaspoons extra-virgin olive oil
Juice of 1 lemon, or more to taste
1 tablespoon finely chopped flat-leaf parsley
1 teaspoon coarse salt
½ teaspoon freshly ground white pepper
¼ teaspoon cayenne pepper
1 ripe avocado
2 green onions, green part only, chopped

1. Fire up the grill. When the coals are hot, grill the tomatoes until charred all around. Cool slightly, place in the bowl of a food processor, and process to a puree. Strain through a medium-fine sieve. Discard the seeds and skins. Refrigerate the tomato puree.

2. Coat the grilling rack with cooking spray. Lightly season the chicken breasts with salt and pepper and place on the grill 5 to 6 inches from the coals. Grill about 4 minutes per side, until done. Do not overcook.

3. Remove the chicken to a chopping board and thinly slice. Set aside to cool.

4. In the bowl of the food processor, coarsely puree the cucumber, red onion, celery, and bell pepper. Transfer to a medium bowl, add the tomato puree, garlic, oil, lemon juice, parsley, coarse salt, white pepper, and cayenne and mix well. Chill. Peel and chop the avocado right before serving.

5. Scoop the gazpacho into 4 shallow bowls. In the center of each, make a mound of the chicken breast strips and avocado. Garnish with the green onions.

Serves 4

Nutritional Breakdown: *197 calories, 4.4 g fat—19% calories from fat, 49.3 mg cholesterol, 4 g fiber, 625 mg sodium*

CHICKEN WITH FIG AND PORT WINE SAUCE

This dish can also be made with broiled or baked chicken breasts.

6 large dried figs, chopped, or 8 to 10 fresh figs, peeled and chopped
2 cups port or other sweet wine (such as Marsala)
4 skinless, boneless chicken breast halves (about 1½ pounds), flattened uniformly between plastic wrap to ½ inch thick
Salt and freshly ground white pepper
2 cups Rich Chicken Stock (see page 16)
4 large shallots, chopped
1 garlic clove, finely chopped
½ large onion, thinly sliced
1 teaspoon cornstarch, dissolved in 1 tablespoon cold water

1. In a small saucepan, add the figs with enough wine to cover. Bring to a simmer over medium heat, and immediately remove from the heat. Set aside to soften.
2. Fire up the grill. Lightly coat the grilling rack with cooking spray and place it 4 to 5 inches from the hot coals. Season the chicken breasts with salt and pepper and grill for 3 to 4 minutes per side, or until done through. Remove to a platter and cover with foil to keep warm.
3. Meanwhile, in a medium saucepan over medium-high heat, cook 2 tablespoons of the chicken stock, the shallots, garlic, and onion until well browned and soft, about 5 minutes, adding a bit more stock if necessary. Add the remaining wine to the pan and reduce by half. Add the remaining stock and continue cooking over moderate heat until reduced by one third, about 5 minutes. Remove the pan from the heat.
4. Add the cornstarch mixture to the pan and cook over low heat until the sauce thickens, about 1 minute. Add the figs and wine and continue cooking over medium-low heat, stirring constantly, about 1 to 2 minutes more. Adjust the seasoning with salt and pepper to taste.
5. Place the chicken breasts on 4 warmed plates and spoon equal amounts of the sauce over them. Serve hot.

Serves 4

Nutritional Breakdown: *513 calories, 3.7 g fat—7% calories from fat, 99.7 mg cholesterol, 4.2 g fiber, 835 mg sodium*

GRILLED CHICKEN BURGERS WITH TOMATO CHUTNEY

Several flavor combinations are particularly delicious in a grilled, low-fat chicken breast burger: Try freshly grated gingerroot, soy sauce, and cilantro as alternative seasonings to the recipe below, and exchange the tomato for mango chutney. While the grill is hot, throw on some asparagus and green onions to serve on the side. Before grilling, coat the vegetables very lightly with olive oil.

2 pounds ground skinless, boneless chicken breasts
¾ cup fresh bread crumbs (from day-old French or sourdough loaf; see pages 12–13)
3 tablespoons finely chopped flat-leaf parsley
½ cup chopped green onion, white and green parts
Salt and freshly ground white pepper
1½ teaspoons grated lemon zest
4 tablespoons Tomato chutney (available in specialty stores and some supermarkets)

1. Fire up the grill or hibachi. Lightly coat the grilling rack with cooking spray and place it 4 to 5 inches from the hot coals.
2. In a large mixing bowl, combine the ground chicken breasts, bread crumbs, parsley, green onion, salt, pepper, and lemon zest and mix to combine well. Shape into four to six rounded patties.
3. Place the burgers on the rack over the hot coals and grill for 5 to 7 minutes per side, or until done. *Do not overcook.* Serve with a tablespoon of tomato chutney on the side.

Serves 4 to 6

Nutritional Breakdown: *329 calories, 3.9 g fat—11% calories from fat, 131 mg cholesterol, 1.3 g fiber, 313 mg sodium*

Use a Handful of Herbs as a Basting Brush

It looks great and this natural brush imparts its own particular flavor in the process. To make a natural herb brush, line up the herbs in even 6- to 7-inch lengths. Wind raffia or kitchen string around one end and tie to form a handle. Dip the brush in the basting or barbecue sauce and apply liberally to chicken breasts cooking on the grill.

CARIBBEAN GRILLED CHICKEN

You've heard of "jerk" chicken, haven't you? It's standard barbecue fare on most Caribbean islands. This is a version of that dish, with just as much hot, hot, hot!

1 cup coarsely chopped onion
1 cup coarsely chopped green onion, white and green parts
1–2 Scotch bonnet chilies, stemmed, seeded, and coarsely chopped (or substitute 2 medium jalapeño chilies, halved, seeded, and chopped)
2 teaspoons ground allspice
1 teaspoon cracked black pepper
1 teaspoon dried thyme
1 teaspoon ground nutmeg
1 teaspoon ground cinnamon
1 teaspoon salt
¼ cup packed dark brown sugar
¼ cup fresh orange juice
¼ cup fresh lemon juice
2 tablespoons canola or other vegetable oil
6–8 skinless, boneless chicken breast halves (about 2½–3 pounds)

1. In a blender or the bowl of a food processor fitted with the metal blade, combine the onion, green onion, chilies, allspice, black pepper, thyme, nutmeg, cinnamon, salt, and brown sugar. Process to a coarse paste. With the motor running, pour in the orange and lemon juices and add the oil in a thin stream.

2. Place the chicken breasts in a shallow dish. Pour on the marinade and turn to coat well on all sides. Cover with plastic wrap and marinate for 3 to 4 hours in the refrigerator.

3. Fire up the grill. Lightly coat the grilling rack with cooking spray and place it 5 to 6 inches from the hot coals. Grill the chicken breast for 10 to 12 minutes, turning a few times to prevent burning. Cut open 1 breast to test for doneness. Serve hot or cold.

Serves 6

Nutritional Breakdown: *322 calories, 7.5 g fat—21% calories from fat, 121 mg cholesterol, 1.6 g fiber, 580 mg sodium*

SPICY MEXICAN GRILLED CHICKEN BREASTS WITH SWEET AND HOT CITRUS VINAIGRETTE

This chicken is particularly delicious when served chilled. While the grill is still hot, smoke some tomatoes for a sauce. This is great al fresco party fare and partners wonderfully with traditional mixed greens salads, or coleslaw and potato salad.

¼ cup tomato paste
Juice of 1 lime
1 teaspoon dried chili powder (ancho or pasilla if possible)
1 teaspoon ground cumin
1 teaspoon ground cinnamon
½ teaspoon salt
2 garlic cloves, minced
4 skinless, boneless chicken breast halves (about 1½ pounds)

Vinaigrette
½ cup fresh orange juice
1½ tablespoons fresh lemon juice
1½ tablespoons fresh lime juice
1½ tablespoons finely chopped red onion
⅛ teaspoon dried chili powder (ancho or pasilla if possible)
2 tablespoons red wine vinegar
1 tablespoon balsamic vinegar
1 tablespoon honey
1½ tablespoons extra-virgin olive oil

1. In a small bowl, combine the tomato paste, lime juice, chili powder, cumin, cinnamon, salt, and garlic. Press the ingredients with the back of a wooden spoon to form a smooth paste.
2. Rub the chicken breasts with the paste to coat completely and place in a dish. Cover with plastic wrap and marinate for 2 hours in the refrigerator. Return to room temperature before grilling.
3. To make the vinaigrette, combine the orange, lemon, and lime juices, red onion, chili powder, both vinegars, and the honey in a blender. With the motor running, add the oil in a thin stream and blend until smooth. Transfer to a bowl and set aside.
4. Fire up the grill. Lightly coat the grilling rack with cooking spray and place it 4 to 5 inches from the coals.

Grill the chicken breasts about 5 to 6 minutes per side, or just until done. Place on a serving platter and drizzle 2 tablespoons of the vinaigrette over each chicken breast. Pass the remaining vinaigrette on the side, if desired.

Serves 4

Nutritional Breakdown (includes 2 tablespoons of vinaigrette per serving): *314 calories, 9.4 g fat—25% calories from fat, 98.6 mg cholesterol, 1.7 g fiber, 517 mg sodium*

Quick Marinades

Thai: Juice of 2 limes, 2 tablespoons fish sauce, 3 tablespoons soy sauce, 1 minced shallot, 2–3 tablespoons cold-pressed peanut oil, 3 hot green chilies, such as jalapeños, seeded and minced

Southwestern: Juice of 2 limes, ½ cup tequila, 2 tablespoons olive oil, ½ cup chopped onion, 2 tablespoons chopped fresh cilantro, pinch of salt

Mediterranean: 3 tablespoons olive oil, ¼ cup balsamic vinegar, 1 chopped onion, 5 minced garlic cloves, 1 large chopped tomato, ¼ teaspoon red pepper flakes, 1 tablespoon chopped fresh oregano, 3 tablespoons chopped flat-leaf parsley, pinch of salt and pepper

Indian: ½ cup plain nonfat yogurt, 2 tablespoons vegetable oil, juice of 1 lime, juice of 1 lemon, ½ chopped onion, 3 minced garlic cloves, 2 tablespoons Indian tandoori spice, pinch of salt

Provençal: 1 cup dry white wine, juice of 1 lemon, 1 chopped onion, 1 tablespoon Dijon mustard, 5 tablespoons herbes de Provence, salt and freshly ground black pepper

Chinese: 1 head garlic, cloves peeled and minced; 1 tablespoon plum sauce; ¼ cup dry sherry; 1 tablespoon soy sauce; 1 tablespoon very hot chili paste; 1 tablespoon minced fresh cilantro

Texas: 4 minced garlic cloves, 1 small hot red chili with seeds removed, 1 teaspoon chopped fresh cilantro, ¼ teaspoon ground cumin, ½ teaspoon ground anise seed, pinch of salt, 2 tablespoons brown sugar, 1 tablespoon Worcestershire sauce, 1 cup cider vinegar, 2 cups ketchup, 1–2 tablespoons Tabasco sauce

GRILLED CHICKEN WITH PAPAYA AND MANGO RELISH

Many chicken breast recipes that call for grilling can be converted to broiling. Always preheat the broiler to high at least 10 minutes before cooking the chicken, and use a broiling pan that elevates the breasts above the fat drippings.

Relish

1 cup diced and peeled ripe mango
1 cup diced and peeled ripe papaya
1 cup peeled, seeded, and diced plum tomatoes
⅓ cup finely chopped red onion
¼ cup finely chopped green onion, green part only
1 tablespoon finely chopped fresh cilantro
1 tablespoon extra-virgin olive oil
¼ cup fresh lime juice
½–1 small jalapeño pepper, seeded and finely minced
Pinch of salt

Marinade and Barbecue Sauce

1 can (8 ounces) crushed tomatoes
1 cup cubed and peeled ripe mango
2 tablespoons white wine vinegar
3 tablespoons honey
2 tablespoons smoky canned chipotle chilies in adobo (available in Latin markets and some supermarkets)
Salt and freshly ground black pepper
4 skinless, boneless chicken breast halves (about 1½ pounds), pounded between plastic wrap to ½ inch thick

1. To make the relish, in a small glass or pottery bowl, combine the mango, papaya, tomato, red onion, green onion, cilantro, oil, lime juice, jalapeño to taste, and salt. Set aside.

2. To prepare the chicken, in a blender or a food processor, combine the tomatoes, mango, vinegar, honey, and chilies and process until smooth. Adjust the seasoning with salt and pepper.

3. Place the chicken in a glass dish. Pour on the marinade and turn to coat all sides. Cover with plastic wrap and marinate for 1 hour in the refrigerator.

4. Meanwhile, fire up the grill. Lightly coat the grilling rack with cooking spray and place it 5 to 6 inches from the hot coals. Grill the chicken, basting again with the marinade if necessary, about 4 to 5 minutes per side, or until done.

Turn twice during grilling so the marinade doesn't burn. Serve hot or at room temperature with 2 tablespoons of the relish. Serve the remaining relish on the side.

Serves 4 to 6

Nutritional Breakdown (includes 2 tablespoons of relish per serving): *340 calories, 6 g fat—16% calories from fat, 98.6 mg cholesterol, 3.3 g fiber, 323 mg sodium*

BLACKENED CAJUN CHICKEN

This is the Cajun version of a simple grilled chicken breast. Sweet and spicy, with lots of rich, crusty barbecue color on the outside of the chicken.

2½ cups fresh orange juice
4 skinless, boneless chicken breast halves (about 1½ pounds)
2–3 tablespoons Louisiana or Cajun spice mix
2 teaspoons balsamic vinegar

1. In a small but heavy saucepan, over high heat, boil 2 cups of the orange juice until reduced by half, about 5 to 6 minutes. Set aside in the saucepan.
2. In a shallow glass dish, place the chicken breasts along with the remaining ½ cup orange juice. Cover with plastic wrap and marinate for 30 minutes at room temperature or 1 hour in the refrigerator.
3. Meanwhile, fire up the grill. Lightly coat the grilling rack with cooking spray and place 5 to 6 inches from the coals.
4. Remove the chicken from the marinade. Pat dry with paper towels. Rub the spice mix on to coat well.
5. When the coals are very hot and coated with a layer of white ash, grill the chicken for 10 to 12 minutes, turning twice, or until the chicken is blackened on the outside and done throughout. Cut open 1 breast to test for doneness.
6. Add the balsamic vinegar to the reserved reduced orange juice and, over high heat, reduce to a syrupy sauce, about 3 to 4 minutes.
7. Drizzle the sauce over the grilled, blackened chicken breast. Serve hot or at room temperature.

Serves 4

Nutritional Breakdown: *269 calories, 2.8 g fat—10% calories from fat, 98.6 mg cholesterol, 0.6 g fiber, 1,714 mg sodium*

SMOKED CHICKEN SALAD WITH HORSERADISH SAUCE AND APPLE SLAW

If smoking your own chicken breasts is out of the question but you like the sound of this salad, most specialty take-out delis carry smoked chicken breasts that are extremely moist and flavorful.

4 skinless, boneless chicken breast halves (about 1½ pounds), or 4 smoked chicken breast halves (available in specialty markets and delis)
Fruitwood charcoal and chips: apple, cherry, or peach (see page 133 for instructions)

Dressing
1 tablespoon finely grated fresh horseradish, or 1 tablespoon bottled, rinsed and drained
⅓ cup low-fat or nonfat plain yogurt
⅓ cup low-fat or nonfat sour cream
Pinch of salt
Pinch of freshly ground white pepper
1–2 teaspoons fresh lemon juice

Apple Slaw
4 tart green apples, peeled, cored, and grated
¼ cup fresh lemon juice
2 stalks celery, very thinly sliced
½ cup finely chopped parsley leaves
2 small shallots, very finely sliced
1 teaspoon celery seed
½ cup plain nonfat yogurt
4 or more red leaf lettuce leaves

1. To smoke the chicken breasts, see page 133 for smoking instructions and tips, and finishing the breasts in the oven.
2. To make the dressing, in a small bowl, whisk together the horseradish, yogurt, sour cream, salt, pepper, and lemon juice until well combined. Adjust the seasonings. Refrigerate until ready to use.
3. To make the apple slaw, in a mixing bowl, combine the apples, lemon juice, celery, parsley, shallots, celery seed, and yogurt. Toss to mix well. Refrigerate.
4. Cut the chicken breasts in thin slices on the diagonal.
5. Divide the lettuce among 4 plates. Top equal amounts of the apple slaw. Arrange the smoked chicken breast slices around the lettuce and drizzle on 1 tablespoon of the horseradish dress-

ing. Pass the remaining dressing, if desired, and the pepper mill.

Serves 4

Simple Tips for Smoking

The Barbecue/Smoker: Use only a barbecue/smoker with an attached, tight-fitting hooded cover or lid. Do not attempt to improvise; use only a barbecue that is also designated as a smoker. Place it as far away from the house or open windows as possible.

The Wood: Use hardwoods *charcoal* such as mesquite (sparingly) and fruitwoods like apple or cherry. Use fruitwood *chips* or small chunks for creating smoke, and grapevine cuttings and fresh herbs to impart flavor. First soak 4 cups of chips in water for 10 minutes, or about 10 chunks for about 30 minutes before adding to the barbecue.

The Fire: If grilling foods first, remember to make the grilling fire with hardwood charcoal as recommended above, and *never with commercial charcoal briquettes,* which are made with less than desirable substances for smoking and impart a bad flavor. When the embers die down, it is time to assemble your barbecue/smoker with the food, chips, and other ingredients as desired.

Nutritional Breakdown (includes 1 tablespoon of dressing per serving): *320 calories, 2.9 g fat—8% calories from fat, 99.5 mg cholesterol, 3.3 g fiber, 172 mg sodium*

The Steps for Smoking

1. Push the embers on the bottom to one side of the barbecue/smoker.

2. Place a pan of water, wine, beer, or water scented with liquor such as bourbon or whiskey just opposite the smoldering charcoal, also in the bottom of the barbecue/smoker.

3. Fit the grilling rack in place.

4. Arrange the food on the grilling rack over the pan of liquid.

5. Toss a few of the soaked hardwood chips or chunks on to the charcoal and slam down the cover as smoke almost instantly begins to billow up . . . and can get in your eyes. It's not good to breathe in the strong smoke either.

Smoking Time: The temperature inside the barbecue should be around 200° F., or slightly less. The smoking time should be about 30 to 40 minutes; the chicken should be pink throughout, but not raw looking. Test one breast by cutting it open. After the chicken breasts have been smoked, immediately place them in a conventional oven preheated to 325° F. and bake for 8 to 10 minutes, or until done.

DALLAS-STYLE BARBECUED CHICKEN

This recipe for a delicate but very tasty version of Texas barbecue sauce makes enough for a "whole lot" of chicken breasts, so you may want to freeze half of the sauce for another night later on in the hot season.

Barbecue Sauce

2–4 garlic cloves, coarsely chopped
1 small dried hot red chili, stem and seeds removed
1 tablespoon chopped fresh cilantro
¾ teaspoon ground cumin
½ teaspoon fennel seed
½ teaspoon salt
2 tablespoons dark brown sugar
1 tablespoon Worcestershire sauce
1 cup cider vinegar
2 cups ketchup
2–3 teaspoons Tabasco sauce

6–8 skinless, boneless chicken breast halves (about 3 pounds)

1. In a blender or the bowl of a food processor fitted with a metal blade, process the garlic, chili, cilantro, cumin, fennel seed, salt, brown sugar, and Worcestershire sauce until smooth.

2. Transfer the mixture to a small saucepan and add the vinegar and ketchup. Bring to a boil, reduce the heat, and simmer, uncovered, for 25 to 30 minutes. Add the Tabasco sauce. Set aside and cool to room temperature.

3. Place the chicken breasts in a glass dish. Pour on the sauce and generously coat all sides. Marinate for 30 minutes at room temperature or up to 1 hour in the refrigerator.

4. Meanwhile, fire up the grill. Lightly coat the grilling rack with cooking spray and place it 5 to 6 inches from the hot coals. Grill the chicken breasts, basting once and turning several times so the chicken doesn't burn, for 12 to 15 minutes, or until done throughout. Cut open 1 breast to test for doneness. Serve hot or at room temperature.

Serves 4 to 8, makes about 2 cups of barbecue sauce

Nutritional Breakdown: *541 calories, 4.8 g fat—8% calories from fat, 197 mg cholesterol, 1.9 g fiber, 2,009 mg sodium*

THAI CHICKEN SATAY WITH PEANUT DIPPING SAUCE

4 skinless, boneless chicken breast halves (about 1½ pounds), pounded between plastic wrap to ¼ inch thick (or use chicken breast tenders)
25 or more 6-inch wooden skewers, soaked in water for 1 hour
Juice of 1 lemon
Salt and freshly ground black pepper

Dipping Sauce

3 tablespoons unsalted smooth peanut butter (natural-style, oil drained off, if possible)
1 tablespoon tahini (sesame paste)
4 tablespoons reduced-sodium soy sauce or tamari
4 to 5 tablespoons low-fat or nonfat yogurt
2 tablespoons dark or light brown sugar
2 large garlic cloves, finely minced
2 tablespoons rice wine or white wine vinegar
⅛ teaspoon crushed red pepper, or more to taste
1½ tablespoons finely chopped toasted peanuts for garnish

1. Cut the flattened chicken into 1 × 4-inch strips and thread on the skewers. Sprinkle with the lemon juice and season with salt and pepper. Set aside.

2. To make the dipping sauce, in a small bowl, whisk together the peanut butter, tahini, soy sauce, 4 tablespoons of the yogurt, the brown sugar, garlic, vinegar, and red pepper until very smooth. Add the remaining 1 tablespoon yogurt for a thinner sauce. Cover with plastic wrap and let stand for 1 hour before serving.

3. Fire up the hibachi or grill. Lightly coat the grilling rack with cooking spray and place it 4 to 5 inches from the hot coals. Grill the chicken skewers for 2 minutes per side, or until done. Do not overcook. Serve hot off the grill with the dipping sauce and chopped peanuts.

Serves 6 to 8 as an appetizer

Nutritional Breakdown: *170 calories, 5.7 g fat—30% calories from fat, 49.5 mg cholesterol, 0.7 g fiber, 469 mg sodium*

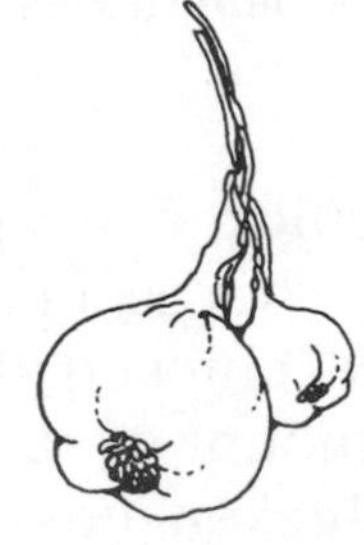

CHICKEN BREASTS WITH ROASTED ONION MARMALADE

4 skinless, boneless chicken breast halves (about 1½ pounds)
¼ cup mixed chopped fresh herbs (such as parsley, chervil, tarragon, and basil)
¼ cup apple juice
¼ cup Defatted Chicken Stock (see page 18)
2 large garlic cloves, thinly sliced
Salt and freshly ground white pepper

Onion Marmalade

1 large red onion, unpeeled and halved
1 large sweet onion (such as Vidalia, Maui, or Walla Walla), unpeeled and halved
1 teaspoon vegetable oil
2 garlic cloves, finely minced
½ cup port wine, or other sweet wine
½ cup full-bodied red wine (such as Merlot)
3 tablespoons balsamic vinegar
¼ cup orange juice
¼ cup honey
1 teaspoon grated orange zest
1 teaspoon grated lemon zest
Pinch of salt

1. Place the chicken in a glass dish. Sprinkle on the herbs. In a cup, combine the apple juice, chicken stock, garlic, and a scant amount of salt and pepper. Pour on the chicken, cover tightly with plastic wrap, and marinate for 1 hour.

2. Meanwhile, make the marmalade. Preheat the oven to 450°F. Place the onion cut side down on a baking sheet lightly coated with cooking spray. Bake for 45 to 50 minutes, or until tender. Cool, peel, and chop coarsely.

3. In a heavy skillet lightly coated with cooking spray, heat the oil. Add the garlic and chopped onions and cook over medium heat for 2 minutes, stirring constantly. Add the port, reduce the heat, and cook for 5 minutes to reduce slightly.

4. To the skillet, add the red wine, vinegar, orange juice, honey, both zests, and salt and continue cooking until the liquid is syrupy and the onions are tender, about 8 to 10 minutes. Transfer to a serving bowl. Cool to room temperature.

5. Drain the chicken breasts and reserve the marinade. Fire up the grill (or preheat the broiler). Lightly coat the grilling rack with cooking spray and place it 5 to 6 inches from the hot coals. Grill (or broil) the chicken for 4 to 5 minutes per side, or until the chicken is done through. Remove from the grill and keep warm.

6. Meanwhile, simmer the reserved marinade in a saucepan until reduced by half, about 6 minutes. Adjust the seasoning with salt and pepper to taste. Place the chicken on a platter, pour on the sauce, and serve with equal amounts of the onion marmalade on the side.

Serves 4

Nutritional Breakdown: *345 calories, 3.9 g fat—10% calories from fat, 115 mg cholesterol, 1.4 g fiber, 227 mg sodium*

ASIAN ORANGE-GLAZED CHICKEN BREASTS

1 cup orange juice
1 tablespoon dark brown sugar
1 tablespoon grated orange zest
2 tablespoons rice wine vinegar
2 tablespoons reduced-sodium soy sauce or tamari
2 teaspoons canola or olive oil
2 medium garlic cloves, finely minced
1 tablespoon finely minced peeled fresh ginger
¼ teaspoon freshly ground white pepper
¼ teaspoon crushed star anise
4 skinless, boneless chicken breast halves (about 1½ pounds), pounded between plastic wrap to ½ inch thick

1. Reduce the orange juice by half in a small saucepan over medium heat, about 4 to 5 minutes. Cool.
2. In a jar with a tight-fitting lid, combine the orange juice, brown sugar, zest, vinegar, soy sauce, oil, garlic, ginger, pepper, and star anise. Shake until well mixed.
3. Place the chicken breasts in a shallow dish. Pour the marinade over the chicken breasts and turn to coat well. Cover tightly with plastic wrap and marinate for 2 to 3 hours in the refrigerator. Let come to room temperature before grilling. Drain off the marinade.
4. Fire up the grill. Lightly coat the grilling rack with cooking spray and place it 5 to 6 inches from the hot coals. Grill the chicken breasts, about 5 to 6 minutes per side, or until done through.

Serves 4

Nutritional Breakdown: *258 calories, 4.6 g fat—17% calories from fat, 98.6 mg cholesterol, 0.3 g fiber, 518 mg sodium*

CRISPY GINGER CHICKEN WITH SAKE DIPPING SAUCE

This is perfect for hors d'oeuvres.

20 pieces melba or other reduced-fat dry crisp toasts, finely crushed into crumbs (about 1½ cups)
½ teaspoon ground ginger
1 tablespoon grated peeled fresh ginger
½ teaspoon salt
¼ teaspoon freshly ground white pepper
2 large egg whites
1 tablespoon sake (Japanese rice wine)
1 pound chicken breast "tenders" or fillets, or 1 pound skinless, boneless chicken breasts, pounded between plastic wrap to ½ inch thick and cut into 1 × 4-inch strips

Sake Sauce

¼ cup reduced-sodium soy sauce or tamari
¼ cup sake (Japanese rice wine)
2 tablespoons Defatted Chicken Stock (see page 18)
1 teaspoon sugar
1 teaspoon grated peeled fresh ginger
½ small garlic clove, finely minced

1 tablespoon unsalted butter, melted

1. Preheat the oven to 375°F. Lightly coat a foil-lined broiler pan with cooking spray.

2. In a large plastic bag, combine the toast crumbs, ground ginger, fresh ginger, salt, and pepper. Shake to mix, pour on a plate, and make an even layer.

3. In a shallow dish, whisk the egg whites and sake together until frothy. Dip the chicken fillets in the egg and coat on all sides, letting the excess drip back into the dish.

4. Coat the fillets with the crumbs, firmly pressing them into the surface.

5. To make the sauce, in a small saucepan, combine the soy sauce or tamari, the sake, stock, sugar, ginger, and garlic. Heat slowly over low heat, about 1 to 2 minutes, until the sugar dissolves. Place in a small serving bowl. Set aside.

6. Place the chicken breast fillets in the broiling pan. Put the melted butter in a sprayer and spray to coat the fillets, or gently dab the melted butter on the fillets with a pastry brush. Place the fillets in the oven and bake for 3 to 4 minutes, or until done; do not turn. Remove from the oven.

7. Turn the broiler to high. Finish cooking the chicken in the broiler for 30 seconds per side. Serve hot or warm with dipping sauce.

Serves 4 as a main course, or 6 as an appetizer

Nutritional Breakdown: *281 calories, 5.1 g fat—18% calories from fat, 73.5 mg cholesterol, 1.7 g fiber, 1,410 mg sodium*

SMOKED CHICKEN SALAD WITH GOLDEN CAVIAR SAUCE

You can smoke your own chicken breasts for this salad, just use the instructions on page 133.

1 jar (2 ounces) American golden caviar
¾ cup low-fat sour cream
1 teaspoon Dijon mustard, or more to taste
2 tablespoons very finely chopped fresh chives
5 large lemon wedges
4 cups washed mixed salad greens
4 smoked skinless, boneless chicken breast halves (about 1½ pounds, available in specialty markets and deli)
Salt and freshly ground white pepper

1. In a small bowl, gently fold together the caviar, sour cream, mustard, and 1 tablespoon of the chopped chives. Transfer to a serving bowl and refrigerate until ready to serve.

2. Place one lemon wedge on 4 individual plates and divide the salad greens.

3. On a wooden cutting board, thinly slice the smoked chicken breasts. Season with salt and pepper to taste. Arrange the slices over the greens. Splash the chicken breast slices with a few drops of fresh lemon juice from the remaining lemon wedge.

4. Place 2 tablespoons of the caviar sauce on top of the slices. Serve with the remaining sauce on the side, if desired. Garnish with the remaining 1 tablespoon chopped chives. Pass the pepper mill.

Serves 4

Nutritional Breakdown (includes 2 tablespoons of sauce per serving): *261 calories, 5.4 g fat—19% calories from fat, 153 mg cholesterol, 0.7 g fiber, 2,698 mg sodium*

CARIBE-STYLE CHICKEN BREASTS

4 skinless, boneless chicken breast halves (about 1½ pounds), pounded between plastic wrap to flatten slightly
Salt and freshly ground black pepper
3 garlic cloves, minced
3 shallots, minced
1 cup fresh orange juice
⅓ cup dark Caribbean rum
½ cup white wine
⅓ cup fresh lime juice
1 tablespoon reduced-sodium soy sauce or tamari
1 teaspoon ground ginger
2 tablespoons chopped fresh flat-leaf parsley

1. Place the chicken breasts in a shallow glass dish. Season with salt and pepper.
2. In a small bowl, stir together the garlic, shallots, orange juice, rum, wine, lime juice, soy sauce, ginger, and parsley. Pour over the chicken, cover with plastic wrap, and refrigerate.
3. Drain the chicken and reserve the marinade. Fire up the grill (or preheat the broiler). Lightly coat the grilling rack with cooking spray and place it 5 to 6 inches from the hot coals. Grill (or broil) the chicken for 4 to 5 minutes per side, or until the chicken is done throughout. Remove from the grill and keep warm.
4. Meanwhile, in a small heavy saucepan, boil the reserved marinade until reduced by one-third, about 8 minutes, and serve with the chicken breasts.

Serves 4

Nutritional Breakdown: *305 calories, 2.3 g fat—7% calories from fat, 98.6 mg cholesterol, 0.4 g fiber, 319 mg sodium*

It May Be Raining on the Grill . . . but the Broiler Is Dry

Preheat the broiler for at least 15 minutes before beginning to cook. The breast meat should be at least ¾ inch thick. If it's thinner there is a good chance it will dry out too quickly. Place the chicken breasts in a shallow broiler-proof pan and add just enough liquid—such as wine, vermouth, lemon juice, or water—to keep the meat from drying out. (Marinated chicken breasts are more likely to stay moist throughout broiling.) Set the broiling grill so the chicken breasts are from 5 to 6 inches from the direct flame. Turn once during cooking, about 4 minutes on each side, until just cooked through. Don't overcook!

BALSAMIC CHICKEN SKEWERS

The taste of balsamic vinegar has become very popular in the past few years. No wonder it's a staple in our pantries. Fill up the grill and baste the chicken skewers with this marinade and throw on some skewered seasonal vegetables as well.

½ cup dry white wine
½ cup Defatted Chicken Stock (see page 18)
½ cup balsamic vinegar
¼ cup dark raisins, chopped
1 tablespoon canola or extra-virgin olive oil
1 tablespoon grated orange zest
1 tablespoon grated lemon zest
2 teaspoons chopped fresh tarragon
4 skinless, boneless chicken breast halves (about 1½ pounds), flattened between plastic wrap uniformly and cut into 2½-inch chunks
20 or more 6-inch wooden skewers, soaked in water for 1 hour
Salt and freshly ground black pepper

1. Fire up the grill or preheat the broiler.
2. In a small saucepan, combine the wine, chicken stock, balsamic vinegar, raisins, oil, both zests, and tarragon and bring to a boil. Reduce the mixture over medium heat by two thirds, about 8 to 10 minutes. Cool. Place in a blender and blend until smooth.
3. Thread each chicken chunk onto 2 parallel skewers placed 1 inch apart so that the meat stays flat on the grill. Lightly season with salt and pepper. Place the skewered chicken in a shallow dish. Pour the marinade over the chunks and marinate for about 20 minutes.
4. Lightly coat the grilling rack with cooking spray and place it 5 to 6 inches from the hot coals.
5. Grill (or broil) the skewered chicken for 4 to 5 minutes per side, or until done throughout. Baste during cooking with the marinade, if desired. Serve on the skewers hot or at room temperature.

Serves 4

Nutritional Breakdown: *272 calories, 5.7 g fat—19% calories from fat, 98.6 mg cholesterol, 0.5 g fiber, 210 mg sodium*

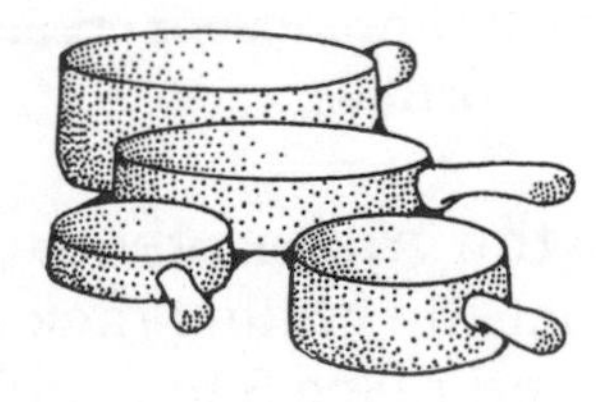

SOFT TACOS FILLED WITH GRILLED CHICKEN AND VEGETABLES

These are great served buffet style.

4 skinless, boneless chicken breast halves (about 1½ pounds), pounded between plastic wrap to ¼ inch thick
Salt and freshly ground black pepper
1 red onion, finely chopped
1 red bell pepper, roasted and seeded (see page 92), cut into julienne
1 yellow bell pepper, roasted and seeded (see page 92), cut into julienne
2 garlic cloves, finely minced
1 cup cooked black beans, drained and rinsed
1 cup julienne-cut jicama
2 cups fresh cilantro leaves
2 tablespoons red wine vinegar
1 tablespoon fresh lime juice
1 tablespoon fresh lemon juice
3 tablespoons fresh orange juice
1 teaspoon honey
1 teaspoon ground coriander
2 tablespoons extra-virgin olive oil
1 tablespoon corn or other vegetable oil
¼ cup nonfat or low-fat sour cream
8 6-inch flour tortillas

1. Fire up the grill or preheat the broiler. Coat the grilling rack with cooking spray and place 5 to 6 inches from the hot coals. Season the chicken with salt and pepper. Cook for 2 to 3 minutes per side, or until done throughout. Cut in thin strips and set aside.

2. In a mixing bowl, combine ½ of the chopped red onion, the bell peppers, ½ of the minced garlic, the black beans, jicama, and ¼ cup of the cilantro leaves. Toss just to mix.

3. In a blender, place the remaining garlic, red onion, and cilantro, the vinegar, lime, lemon, and orange juices, honey, and coriander and process until smooth. With the motor running, add both oils in a thin stream until blended. Place in a bowl and stir in the sour cream. Season with salt and pepper to taste.

4. Pour the vinaigrette over the black bean mixture and toss to mix well.

5. Place an equal amount of the chicken and black bean mixture in the center of each tortilla and roll tightly. Serve at room temperature.

Serves 4

Nutritional Breakdown: *770 calories, 20.9 g fat—25% calories from fat, 98.6 mg cholesterol, 9.5 g fiber, 672 mg sodium*

PLUM-BASTED CHICKEN BREASTS ON THYME COUSCOUS

This recipe was influenced by one from Chef Peter Roelant of the Four Oaks in Los Angeles.

Marinade and Chicken Breasts

¼ cup Chinese plum sauce
¼ cup ketchup
Juice of 1 lime
1 tablespoon fresh grated horseradish, or rinsed and drained bottled horseradish
4 skinless, boneless chicken breast halves (about 1½ pounds), pounded between plastic wrap to ½ inch thick
1 tablespoon extra-virgin olive oil
Salt and freshly ground black pepper
1 small tomato, peeled and diced for garnish
1 tablespoon finely chopped parsley for garnish

Couscous

2 cups bottled spring water
1 teaspoon fresh thyme leaves
1 medium carrot, peeled and finely diced
¼ onion, finely chopped
1 small tomato, peeled and diced
½ cup instant couscous
1 tablespoon extra-virgin olive oil
Salt and freshly ground black pepper

1. In a small mixing bowl, combine the plum sauce, ketchup, lime juice, and horseradish.

2. Brush the chicken with the 1 tablespoon of oil and season with salt and pepper. Brush on the plum sauce mixture and set aside to marinate for 30 minutes.

3. Meanwhile, to make the couscous, in a small saucepan, bring the water, thyme, carrot, onion, and tomato to a boil.

4. Place the couscous in a mixing bowl. Pour on the boiling water and vegetables, cover tightly with plastic wrap, and let stand for 10 minutes, or until the water is completely absorbed.

5. Fire up the grill. Lightly coat the grilling rack with cooking spray and place it 5 to 6 inches from the hot coals. Grill the chicken for 5 to 6 minutes per side, or until done throughout.

6. Fluff the couscous with a fork to mix. Drizzle on the 1 tablespoon oil and toss gently. Season lightly with salt and pepper to taste. Set aside.

7. Place equal amounts of the couscous mixture in the center of 4 warmed dinner plates and make a well in the center for the chicken breast pieces.

8. Slice each breast across the grain into ½-inch-thick medallions and arrange in the center of the couscous. Sprinkle diced tomato and chopped parsley over the chicken and couscous. Serve hot or warm.

Serves 4

Nutritional Breakdown: *422 calories, 9.2 g fat—20% calories from fat, 98.6 mg cholesterol, 2.2 g fiber, 462 mg sodium*

CRISPY CHICKEN CUTLETS ON GARLIC MASHED POTATOES

5 whole garlic cloves, peeled
6 medium boiling potatoes, peeled and diced
4 cups nonfat milk
1 tablespoon unsalted butter
1 teaspoon salt
1 teaspoon freshly ground white pepper
4 skinless, boneless chicken breast halves (about 1½ pounds), pounded between plastic wrap to ¼ inch thick
1 tablespoon dried bread crumbs
1 tablespoon finely grated Parmesan cheese
2 tablespoons finely chopped flat-leaf parsley

1. Preheat the broiler.
2. In a large saucepan or stockpot, bring the garlic, potatoes, and milk to a boil. Reduce the heat to a simmer and cook until tender, about 10 to 12 minutes. Drain, reserving the milk.
3. Mash the potatoes and garlic until smooth, adding the reserved milk as needed to make them fluffy. Season with salt and pepper to taste. Keep warm.
4. Meanwhile, broil the chicken about 2 to 3 minutes per side, just until done throughout. Toss the bread crumbs and the Parmesan together and sprinkle over the cutlets. Return to the broiler for 30 seconds or just until the topping gets crispy. Cover with foil to keep warm.
5. Make a bed of mashed potatoes on 4 individual plates. Place a chicken breast on each plate and sprinkle with the parsley.

Serves 4

Nutritional Breakdown: *494 calories, 6.2 g fat—12% calories from fat, 112 mg cholesterol, 2.9 g fiber, 824 mg sodium*

SMOKED CHICKEN BREASTS AND CHOPPED SWEET ONION SALAD

Three types of sweet onions—Maui, Vidalia, and Walla Walla—are readily available in supermarkets and organic grocery stores, as well as at local farmers' markets. Use any of them in this salad.

2–3 large ripe tomatoes (or 6 to 8 plum), chopped
⅔ cup chopped sweet onion
4 green onions, white and green parts, chopped
2 cups (about ¾ pound) smoked chicken breast chunks (to smoke your own chicken breasts, see page 133)
1 tablespoon canola or corn oil
1 tablespoon extra-virgin olive oil
3 tablespoons fresh lemon juice
3 tablespoons fresh orange juice
Salt and freshly ground black pepper
8 cups mixed salad greens (such as romaine, curly endive, red leaf or Boston lettuce, mâche, and radicchio)

1. In a medium mixing bowl, combine the tomatoes, onion, green onions, and chicken chunks.
2. In a glass jar with a tight-fitting lid, combine both oils, 2 tablespoons of the lemon juice, and 2 tablespoons of the orange juice and shake to mix well.
3. Drizzle the dressing on the chicken and onions and toss gently to combine. Adjust the seasoning with salt and pepper.
4. Place the salad greens in a large mixing bowl. Drizzle the remaining 1 tablespoon each orange and lemon juices over the lettuce, season lightly with salt and pepper, and toss gently to mix. Arrange on 4 large salad plates and divide the chicken breast mixture among the plates.

Serves 4

Nutritional Breakdown: *193 calories, 6.6 g fat—30% calories from fat, 34.9 mg cholesterol, 3.1 g fiber, 1,238 mg sodium*

Stove Top

Variety is a key word in this collection of low-fat chicken breast recipes. This is undoubtedly the "every cooks" chapter, offering recipes you will be pleased to know are approved and improved for low-fat cooking or eating. A good example is the White Wine Coq au Vin (page 169) with a creamy finish of nonfat sour cream. You'll discover a robust ragout of interesting mushrooms, and a sweetly satisfying one with fruit, both accompanied by (guess!) delicious low-fat chicken breasts. And, there's a recipe for the most popular Chinese appetizer, Pot Stickers (page 152), filled with a delicate ginger–chicken breast filling and served with a traditional dipping sauce. When there's a brunch on the horizon, there's Southwestern Chicken Hash (page 160) with salsa on the side. A few Louisiana favorites, like Creole-style Chicken Gumbo (page 167), are thrown in for an extra good and spicy balance, and there's even a recipe for hearty Spicy Chicken and 3-Bean Chili (page 163). On a chilly night, rely on the recipe for Herbed Chicken Fricassee (page 171), which can be easily adjusted as seasonal ingredients change.

Obviously, this is also the "everyday" chapter because there are so many easy recipes waiting to be discovered. So, get a nice big nonstick skillet and plan on cooking your way from one end of this chapter to the other. And keep reminding yourself that, yes, these are low-fat recipes, even though the food tastes really, really rich and good.

BARLEY RISOTTO WITH CHICKEN AND VEGETABLES

This wonderful risotto is influenced by a recipe created for the Canyon Ranch Spa by Joachim Splichal. Always make risotto in small batches, to serve no more than 6—even barley risotto!

1 (6–8 ounces) skinless, boneless chicken breast half (preferably free range)
1 tablespoon extra-virgin olive oil
3 tablespoons finely chopped onion
3 tablespoons diced carrot
3 tablespoons diced leek, white part only
3 tablespoons diced celery
¼ cup Rich Chicken Stock (see page 16)
3 cups cooked pearl barley (cooked in ½ water and ½ chicken stock, lightly salted), drained
2 tablespoons finely grated Parmesan cheese
1 cup finely chopped flat-leaf parsley
Salt and freshly ground white pepper

1. Preheat the broiler to high. Broil the chicken breast 4 to 6 minutes per side, or until done. When cool enough to handle, julienne the breast meat. Set aside.

2. In a medium nonstick skillet or sauté pan, heat the oil. Add the onion, carrot, leek, and celery and cook over medium heat until tender. Set the vegetables aside.

3. Add the chicken stock to the pan and deglaze over high heat, scraping up any brown bits, until slightly reduced, about 1 minute. Add the barley and continue cooking until most of the remaining liquid is absorbed, about 3 minutes. Add the vegetables and the shredded chicken and toss to combine. Add the Parmesan, and parsley. Stir just to mix. Season with salt and pepper to taste. Serve in 2 warmed pasta bowls. Pass more Parmesan and the pepper mill on the side.

Serves 2

Nutritional Breakdown: *611 calories, 12.4 g fat—18% calories from fat, 112 mg cholesterol, 13 g fiber, 442 mg sodium*

SPINACH PASTA WITH CHICKEN AND LENTILS

Tiny French puy lentils are widely available, and really delicious. They look very delicate in this or any dish.

¾ cup dried tiny French green puy lentils
1½ cups bottled spring water
Pinch of salt
3 ripe plum tomatoes
3 teaspoons canola or extra-virgin olive oil
1 cup Defatted Chicken Stock (see page 18)
1 pound skinless, boneless chicken breast, cut into thin strips
2 garlic cloves, minced
½ cup finely chopped onion
1 cup packed baby spinach leaves, stemmed and coarsely chopped
Salt and freshly ground black pepper
¾ pound fresh spinach pasta, or ½ pound dried
2 teaspoons balsamic vinegar
1 teaspoon chopped dried oregano
2 tablespoons finely grated Parmesan cheese

1. In a large stockpot, combine the lentils, spring water, and salt. Bring to a boil, reduce the heat to a simmer, and cook for 25 minutes, or until tender. Drain and set aside.

2. Fill the same stockpot with water and bring to a boil. Have a large bowl of ice water available. Blanch the tomatoes for 1 minute, remove with a slotted spoon, and plunge into ice water. Peel, seed, dice, and set aside. Reserve the boiling water in the stockpot over high heat.

3. In a large nonstick skillet, heat 1 teaspoon of oil and 2 tablespoons of the chicken stock. Add the chicken strips and cook over medium heat, tossing and stirring constantly, just until done, about 3 to 4 minutes. Remove with a slotted spoon and set aside.

4. In the same skillet, heat 2 more tablespoons of the chicken stock. Add the garlic and onion and cook over medium heat until caramelized, about 8 to 10 minutes. Drizzle in more stock as needed to keep the garlic and onion from sticking to the skillet. Stir often.

5. In the stockpot of boiling water, blanch the spinach just until wilted, about 30 seconds. Remove with a slotted spoon and drain. Over high heat, reserve the boiling water in the stockpot.

6. To the skillet, add 1 teaspoon of oil,

the lentils, and the remaining chicken stock. Season with salt and pepper. Cover and simmer for 5 minutes. Add the chicken strips and cook over very low heat for 1 minute more, or until the chicken heats through.

7. Meanwhile, lightly salt the boiling water in the stockpot. Cook the pasta to al dente, according to package directions. Drain and transfer to a large mixing bowl. Drizzle on the remaining 1 teaspoon of oil, the balsamic vinegar, oregano, and salt and pepper to taste. Toss gently to mix. Add the spinach, tomatoes, and chicken and lentil mixture, and toss again. Serve in a large warmed pasta bowl, topped with the Parmesan. Pass the pepper mill.

Serves 4

Nutritional Breakdown: *535 calories, 7.6 g fat—13% calories from fat, 68.2 mg cholesterol, 12 g fiber, 367 mg sodium*

CHICKEN IN RED WINE SAUCE WITH PAPPARDELLE PASTA

Pappardelle pasta makes a very special presentation, but other wide, fresh pastas can be substituted. If you have a pasta machine, this is the perfect recipe to make your own. Only a few pappardelle are needed for each serving.

2 tablespoons extra-virgin olive oil
4 skinless, boneless chicken breast halves (about 1½ pounds), cut into bite-size pieces
Salt and freshly ground black pepper
1 tablespoon finely chopped onion
1 tablespoon finely chopped peeled carrot
1 tablespoon finely chopped celery
1½ teaspoons finely chopped fresh sage leaves, or ¾ teaspoon dried
½ teaspoon finely chopped fresh rosemary leaves, or ¼ teaspoon dried
¼ cup full-bodied red wine (such as Cabernet Sauvignon)
¼ cup Rich Chicken Stock (see page 16)
2 ripe tomatoes, peeled, seeded, and diced
¾ pound fresh pappardelle pasta (2–3 pieces per serving)
2 tablespoons finely grated Parmesan
1 tablespoon finely chopped flat-leaf parsley

1. In a large nonstick skillet, heat the oil. Season the chicken pieces with salt and pepper, and cook over moderately high heat, turning frequently, until brown on all sides, about 3 minutes. Transfer to a medium bowl. Set aside.
2. To the same skillet, add the onion, carrot, celery, sage, and rosemary and cook, over medium heat, for 2 minutes. Pour in the wine and chicken stock, lower the heat, and simmer for 1 minute. Stir in the tomatoes, partially cover the pan, and simmer for 5 minutes more.
3. Bring a large pot of lightly salted boiling water to a boil. Add the pasta and cook to al dente, about 4 minutes. Drain. Keep warm.
4. Meanwhile, add the chicken pieces and any juice that has collected in the bowl to the vegetables. Continue cooking, partially covered, for 3 to 5 minutes more, or just until the chicken is done. Season with salt and pepper to taste, remove the chicken, and keep it hot.
5. Add the pasta to the pan and toss gently to coat. Divide among 4 heated pasta bowls and top with pieces of chicken breast. Sprinkle on the Parmesan and parsley. Pass the pepper mill.

Serves 4

Nutritional Breakdown: *627 calories, 11.9 g fat—18% calories from fat, 101 mg cholesterol, 3.8 g fiber, 281 mg sodium*

Recapturing the Comfort of a Creamy White Sauce

Low-fat cooking doesn't have to mean removing all the good-tasting stuff from your diet. I mean, the thought of never having a rich and creamy sauce again just isn't fair. Here's a rich and creamy sauce base to which you can add a pleasantly satisfying amount of finely grated Parmesan cheese, or keep it on the lighter side with a cup of sautéed shallots, tomato bits, and herbs of your choice.

1 tablespoon unsalted butter
1 garlic clove, minced
1 tablespoon flour
1½ cups nonfat milk
3 tablespoons nonfat cream cheese
2 tablespoons freshly chopped flat-leaf parsley
1 teaspoon freshly ground white pepper
Pinch of salt to taste

1. Melt the butter and sauté the garlic.
2. Whisk in the flour and then slowly stir in the milk.
3. Cook for 10 minutes over low heat.
4. Add everything else you want.
5. Immediately pour over anything you like. Sounds "rich," doesn't it?

TOMATO AND GARLIC CHICKEN WITH WILD RICE

4 cups Simple Chicken Stock (see page 15)
1 cup uncooked wild rice, soaked for 30 minutes in hot water and drained
Salt and freshly ground black pepper
4 tablespoons seasoned dried bread crumbs
4 skinless, boneless chicken breast halves (about 1½ pounds)
2 teaspoons extra-virgin olive oil
3 garlic cloves, minced
1 cup chopped onion
1 cup chopped celery
4 tablespoons Rich Chicken Stock (see page 16)
2 cups canned tomatoes, well drained and chopped
1 teaspoon grated lemon zest
1 teaspoon chopped fresh rosemary, or ½ teaspoon dried

1. In a heavy saucepan, bring 4 cups of the stock and 1 cup of water to a boil. Add the rice, lightly salt the water, and stir. Cook, covered, over very low heat for 45 minutes. Remove from the heat, let stand for 15 minutes, and drain thoroughly. Adjust the seasoning with salt and pepper. Set aside.
2. Place the bread crumbs on a plate. Dredge the chicken breasts through the bread crumbs to coat well. Set aside.
3. In a large nonstick skillet or sauté pan lightly coated with cooking spray, heat the oil. Add the chicken breast and cook over medium-high heat until brown, about 3 minutes per side. Remove to a platter and cover with foil to keep warm.
4. To the skillet, add the garlic and onion and cook over medium heat for 2 minutes. Add the celery and the 4 tablespoons of Rich Chicken Stock. Cook over medium heat for 5 minutes. Add the tomatoes, lemon zest, and rosemary and cook, stirring constantly, for 1 minute more. Add the chicken breasts, cover, and simmer until done, about 20 minutes.
5. Rewarm the wild rice.
6. Divide the hot wild rice among 4 warmed shallow bowls. Remove the chicken breasts from the skillet and place in another dish. Spoon the tomatoes and sauce over the rice. Arrange the chicken breasts on the rice. Pass the pepper mill.

Serves 4

Nutritional Breakdown: *284 calories, 5 g fat—16% calories from fat, 98.8 mg cholesterol, 2.2 g fiber, 533 mg sodium*

POT STICKERS WITH CHINESE DIPPING SAUCE

Once prepared, the pot stickers can be frozen on baking sheets, transferred to plastic bags, placed in the freezer, and cooked at a later time for instant appetizers. To eliminate even more of the calories in this already reduced-fat recipe, bake the pot stickers in the oven at 450° F. Sprinkle a baking sheet with a small amount of cornstarch, and cook the pot stickers until nicely browned.

Dipping Sauce

¼ cup reduced-sodium soy sauce or tamari
⅓ cup rice wine vinegar
2 tablespoons thinly sliced green onion, green part only
1 tablespoon freshly grated peeled ginger
2 tablespoons honey
2 tablespoons dry sherry

Pot Stickers

2 teaspoons peanut oil
1 teaspoon light sesame oil
1½ teaspoons freshly grated peeled ginger
1 garlic clove, finely minced
4 tablespoons finely chopped green onion
¼ cup drained, finely chopped water chestnuts
2 tablespoons finely chopped celery
3 tablespoons very finely grated peeled carrot
1 tablespoon dry sherry
1 tablespoon reduced-sodium soy sauce or tamari
2 large egg whites, whisked
½ pound ground skinless, boneless chicken breast
3 teaspoons cornstarch, or more
30–36 wonton wrappers
1 tablespoon canola or vegetable oil
¼ cup spring water, or more

1. To make the dipping sauce, in a small bowl, stir the soy sauce, vinegar, green onion, ginger, honey, and sherry until well mixed. Set aside.
2. In a large nonstick skillet, heat the peanut and sesame oils. Add the ginger and garlic and cook for 1 minute over medium heat. Do not brown. Add the green onion and cook briefly, until tender, about 3 minutes.
3. To a medium mixing bowl, add the ginger and garlic mixture, water chestnuts, celery, carrot, sherry, soy sauce, egg whites, and ground chicken. Mix by hand or with a wooden spoon until well combined.

4. Working quickly on a flat, clean surface sprinkled with the cornstarch, take the wonton wrappers, one at a time from the stack, keeping the rest covered so that they won't dry out. Place about 1 teaspoon of the chicken mixture in the center of the wrapper. Moisten the edges and join in the center to close, pinching the edges together to seal completely. The package will form a half-moon shape. Continue until all the wonton wrappers are filled.

5. In a large nonstick skillet lightly coated with cooking spray, heat half of the canola or other vegetable oil over medium-high heat. Cover the bottom of the skillet with half the pot stickers in a single layer. Cook for 2 to 3 minutes, or until the bottoms are nicely browned. Add 2 tablespoons (or more) of the water and cook, partially covered, until the water has evaporated, the bottoms are crisp, and the wonton dough is done, about 2 minutes more. Remove 1 pot sticker from the pan and cut open to test for doneness. Repeat with the remaining oil, pot stickers, and water.

6. Serve very hot with individual bowls of dipping sauce.

Serves 6 to 8 as an appetizer (makes 30 to 36)

Nutritional Breakdown: *382 calories, 6.3 g fat—15% calories from fat, 29.6 mg cholesterol, 0.4 g fiber, 1,208 mg sodium*

When Wine Meets Food

For the right match, no formalities are necessary. The palate speaks. The synergy makes for an enhanced taste, and the whole becomes greater than the sum of the parts. These days, there are plenty of new mixes and matches in the world of wine and food, and lots of highly personalized wine shops with truly dedicated wine merchants to help you through the maze of wine labels and regional wineries. Here are several hints that work every time: Lightly spiced and herbed chicken breast dishes go so well with Chardonnay and Sauvignon Blanc. When the herbs and spices are rich and pungent, such as with Creole, Caribbean, or Old Country European dishes, choose a Pinot Noir, French Beaujolais, dry Gamay Rosé, or Italian Dolcetto. But remember, when it comes to matching food and wine, it's really a matter of taste. Your taste.

ESCALOPES OF CHICKEN ON SPINACH WITH LEMON AND SHALLOT SAUCE

An "escalope" is a thin slice of lightly pounded meat.

2 teaspoons canola or olive oil
4 cups chiffonnade-cut stemmed spinach
Salt and freshly ground white pepper
4 skinless, boneless chicken breast halves (about 1½ pounds), thickly sliced across the grain at an angle and pounded between plastic wrap to ¼ inch thick
¼ cup all-purpose flour, for dusting
1 tablespoon unsalted butter, melted

Sauce
5 large shallots, finely diced
4 tablespoons fresh lemon juice
1 teaspoon grated lemon zest
¼ cup Rich Chicken Stock (see page 16)
¼ cup dry white wine
1 tablespoon very cold unsalted butter, cut into small pieces
1 tablespoon very finely chopped parsley

1. In a medium nonstick skillet lightly coated with cooking spray, heat the oil. Sauté the spinach quickly over medium-high heat for 2 minutes, shaking the pan back and forth to gently toss while cooking. Season with a scant amount of salt and white pepper and remove to a platter. Cover with foil to keep warm. Reserve the pan.
2. Season the chicken breast slices with a scant amount of salt and pepper. Lightly dust with flour, shaking off any excess until just a trace of flour remains.
3. Brush a large skillet or sauté pan with the melted butter and sauté the chicken escalope over medium-high heat just long enough to cook through, about 2 minutes per side. Test for doneness by cutting into 1 escalope. Do not overcook. Transfer to a plate and cover with foil to keep warm.
4. To make the sauce, add the shallots to the pan in which the spinach was cooked, and cook over medium-high heat for 2 minutes, or just until tender. Add the lemon juice, zest, chicken stock, and wine. Increase the heat to high and reduce by half, about 4 minutes. Remove the pan from the heat, and add the cold

bits of butter one at a time, whisking to incorporate each piece completely before adding the next. Stir in all but 1 teaspoon of the parsley. Adjust the seasoning with salt and white pepper to taste. Do not reheat the sauce.

5. Make a bed of spinach on 4 individual plates and top each with several escalopes. Drizzle on equal amounts of sauce and dust with a scant amount of parsley.

Serves 4

Nutritional Breakdown: *398 calories, 11.6 g fat—27% calories from fat, 148 mg cholesterol, 1.72 g fiber, 274 mg sodium*

Pesto! A Many-Flavored Thing

Create some new low-fat, high-flavored pestos with more than just the standard basil flavor. The best, quickest, easiest way to make them is to toss everything in a mini food processor or blender and process until well minced. Then drizzle in the olive oil (in a thin stream) until the mixture reaches a smooth consistency. Store in small containers in the refrigerator or freezer. Add any of the following pesto combinations to olive oil, garlic, toasted pine nuts, and Parmesan:

Seasonal Mixed Herb Pesto: spinach, flat-leaf parsley, arugula leaves, fresh oregano, thyme, basil, chives, or shallots

Oregano or Sage Pesto: fresh oregano or sage leaves, spinach or watercress, flat-leaf parsley, lemon juice

Sun-Dried Tomato Pesto: dry-packed sun-dried tomatoes (softened in warm white wine), basil, flat-leaf parsley

Serving Suggestions: These pestos are just great tossed with chopped grilled chicken breast pieces and served cold as a salad or warm in a pita, wrapped in a fat-free tortilla, or as part of a pasta dish. Remember, a little goes a long way.

HONEY-MUSTARD CHICKEN WITH MUSHROOM RAGOUT

Mushroom Ragout

1½ tablespoons unsalted butter
4 shallots, thinly sliced
1½ pounds mixed mushrooms (white, oyster, chanterelle, cremini, morel, portobello), sliced
1 cup dry white wine
½ cup Rich Chicken Stock (see page 16)
1 tablespoon chopped fresh tarragon leaves
Salt and freshly ground white pepper

Chicken Breasts

¼ cup dried bread crumbs
4 skinless, boneless chicken breast halves (about 1½ pounds)
1 tablespoon plus 1 teaspoon extra-virgin olive oil
1¼ cups Chardonnay or other dry white wine
1 teaspoon dried savory, crushed, or 2 teaspoons minced parsley
1 teaspoon salt
1 teaspoon freshly ground black pepper
2 tablespoons fresh lemon juice
4 tablespoons mild honey mustard
1 tablespoon honey
½ cup low-fat or nonfat sour cream, at room temperature

1. To prepare the mushrooms, in a large nonstick skillet, melt the butter over medium heat. Add the shallots and cook until tender, about 2 minutes. Add the mushrooms, increase the heat, and cook until the mushroom liquid has evaporated and the mushrooms are brown, about 8 minutes. Add the wine, chicken stock, and tarragon. Bring to a boil and cook until the liquid has almost evaporated, about 15 minutes. Season with salt and pepper. Set aside.

2. Place the bread crumbs on a plate. Dredge the chicken breasts in the crumbs to coat well. Set aside.

3. In a heavy nonstick skillet or sauté pan lightly coated with cooking spray, heat 1 tablespoon of the oil. Add the chicken and cook over moderately high heat until brown, about 3 minutes per side. Add the wine, savory or parsley, salt, and pepper, reduce the heat to a simmer, and cook, covered, until the chicken is tender and done, about 15 minutes more.

4. Remove the chicken to a warmed platter and cover with foil. Reserve the juices in the skillet.

5. To the skillet, add the lemon juice, mustard, honey, and the remaining 1 teaspoon of oil and mix well. Return the chicken to the pan and, over very low heat, warm the chicken through for 2 minutes, basting the chicken with the sauce.

6. Meanwhile, rewarm the mushroom ragout. Remove from the heat and stir in the sour cream. Serve the chicken breasts on 4 warm dinner plates, with the mushroom ragout on the side.

Serves 4

Nutritional Breakdown: *460 calories, 12.1 g fat—24% calories from fat, 110 mg cholesterol, 2.9 g fiber, 734 mg sodium*

Chicken Breasts down for the Calorie Count

Weight Watchers says that 3 ounces of skinless, boneless chicken breast, broiled or grilled plain, has 3 grams of fat. That's all. And it's under 100 calories. Here's an amazing fact: It's OK to grill the chicken with the skin on to keep it moist. Then remove the skin and discard, because it contains 50 percent more calories of all fat!

Top Tools and Perfect Pans

The pans that enhance these recipes are heavy, well-balanced skillets that have a nonstick cooking surface (see page 20). Nonstick surfaces eliminate the need for any unnecessary fats and oils. In addition, a nonstick stove-top grill pan will allow you to cook cutlets and paillards in seconds without having to scrape this especially delicate cut of the chicken breast from the pan. Keep a can of vegetable oil cooking spray around to coat the surface of the pan before cooking without adding fat.

CURRIED CHICKEN WITH CARROT AND ONION

A bowl of fluffy steamed rice is the natural accompaniment for this curry dish. It tends to balance the heat. If you like your curry superhot, just increase the amount of curry powder and crushed red pepper.

1½ cups low-fat buttermilk
1 tablespoon honey
2 teaspoons medium to hot curry powder
1 teaspoon ground cumin
1½ teaspoons arrowroot or cornstarch, dissolved in 1 tablespoon water
Pinch of salt
4 skinless, boneless chicken breast halves (about 1½ pounds), cut into bite-size pieces
6 medium carrots, peeled and cut in matchsticks
1 tablespoon canola or other vegetable oil
1 large onion, finely chopped
1 large garlic clove, finely minced
1½-inch piece peeled fresh ginger, finely minced
¼ teaspoon crushed red pepper
3 cups freshly cooked hot white or brown rice
Freshly ground black pepper

1. In a medium bowl, combine 2 tablespoons of the buttermilk, the honey, 1 teaspoon of the curry powder, the cumin, arrowroot mixture, and salt and whisk to combine. Add the chicken pieces and toss to coat well. Cover with plastic wrap and refrigerate for 2 hours.

2. Have a bowl of ice water available. Cook the carrots in lightly salted boiling water to crisp-tender, about 3 minutes. Quickly plunge them into the bowl of ice water. Drain and set aside.

3. In a large nonstick skillet or sauté pan, heat the oil. Add the onion, garlic, and ginger and cook over medium-high heat for 30 seconds. Stir in the remaining 1 teaspoon curry powder and the crushed red pepper. Add the carrots and continue cooking, about 4 to 5 minutes. Remove and set aside.

4. Meanwhile, drain the chicken pieces and discard the marinade. In the same skillet, over medium-high heat, cook the chicken until brown and done, about 5 to 6 minutes. Remove the chicken with a slotted spoon to a serving plate and cover with foil to keep warm. Set aside.

5. Remove the skillet from the heat and immediately stir in the remaining buttermilk and the carrot mixture. Adjust the seasoning with salt and pepper to taste and warm for 30 seconds. Spoon the sauce over the chicken pieces and serve with the hot rice.

Serves 4

Nutritional Breakdown: *543 calories, 7.3 g fat—12% calories from fat, 102 mg cholesterol, 4.8 g fiber, 249 mg sodium*

CHICKEN, PEAS, AND PASTA

1 cup frozen peas, thawed
1 cup Defatted Chicken Stock (see page 18)
1 cup fresh peas with shoots
1 tablespoon extra-virgin olive oil
1 garlic clove, finely minced
2 tablespoons very finely minced onion
1 pound skinless, boneless chicken breast halves, cut into ⅓-inch strips
Salt and freshly ground black pepper
3 cups uncooked pasta, such as ziti, penne, mostaccioli, or fusilli, cooked al dente according to package directions
¼ cup grated Romano cheese, or more to taste

1. In a blender or food processor, combine the thawed peas and the chicken stock, blending until smooth. Pour through a fine mesh strainer and reserve in a bowl. Discard any residue.
2. In a medium saucepan, bring lightly salted water to a boil. Blanch the fresh peas for 1 minute. Drain and run under cold water. Set aside.
3. In a large nonstick skillet or sauté pan, heat the oil. Add the garlic and cook over medium-high heat, stirring constantly, for 30 seconds. Lower the heat, add the onion, and cook until tender, about 3 minutes. Add the chicken strips and cook over medium-high heat until done, about 3 to 4 minutes. Adjust the seasoning with salt and pepper to taste.
4. To the skillet, add the pureed pea mixture and bring to a boil. Add the pasta and blanched fresh peas and stir to mix well. Cook, stirring constantly, for 2 to 3 minutes, or until the sauce thickens. Stir in the cheese and immediately divide among 4 pasta bowls. Pass the pepper mill.

Serves 4

Nutritional Breakdown: *543 calories, 8.3 g fat—14% calories from fat, 72.2 mg cholesterol, 5.6 g fiber, 924 mg sodium*

SOUTHWESTERN CHICKEN HASH WITH SPICY SALSA

Serve with a corn cake, corn bread, or soft, oven-warmed flour tortillas on the side. (Look for low-fat tortillas.)

Spicy Salsa

1 small serrano or jalapeño chile, peeled, stemmed, and seeded
1 medium red onion, quartered
2 small garlic cloves
2 tomatoes, peeled, seeded, and chopped
2 to 3 tablespoons chopped fresh cilantro
3 teaspoons red wine vinegar, or fresh lemon juice
1 teaspoon salt

Chicken Breast Hash

2 teaspoons canola or corn oil
1 pound coarsely ground skinless, boneless chicken breast
½ cup finely diced green bell pepper
½ cup finely diced red bell pepper
⅓ cup finely diced onion
1 teaspoon chili powder
¼ teaspoon ground cumin
1 cup freshly grilled corn kernels (see page 162 for grilling instructions)

1. To make the salsa, in a mini food processor, chop the chile pepper, onion, and garlic until finely minced. Transfer to a medium bowl. Add the tomatoes, cilantro, vinegar or lemon juice, and salt and stir to mix well. Set aside.
2. In a large nonstick skillet or sauté pan lightly coated with cooking spray, heat 1 teaspoon of the oil. Add the ground chicken breast, and cook over medium heat, stirring constantly, for 3 minutes. Remove the partially cooked chicken from the skillet with a slotted spoon. Set aside in a strainer to drain.
3. In the same skillet, heat the remaining teaspoon of the oil. Add the green and red bell peppers and the onion and cook, stirring constantly, over medium heat until soft. Stir in the chili powder and cumin and cook for 1 minute more.
4. Add the corn, chicken, and half the salsa and mix well. Heat through, continue cooking, partially covered, for 3 minutes more, or until the chicken is done. Top with remaining salsa.

Serves 4

Nutritional Breakdown: *187 calories, 4.1 g fat—20% calories from fat, 65.7 mg cholesterol, 2.1 g fiber, 683 mg sodium*

SMOKED CHICKEN WITH WATERCRESS SAUCE OVER PASTA

3 large garlic cloves, peeled and halved
3 shallots, quartered
4 cups loosely packed watercress leaves
1½ teaspoons Dijon mustard
1 cup nonfat sour cream
2 teaspoons fresh lemon juice
Salt and freshly ground black pepper
2 smoked skinless, boneless chicken breast halves (available in specialty markets and delis, or see the smoking instructions on page 133)
¾ pound dried bow-tie pasta or other pasta
2 teaspoons unsalted butter, melted
2 tablespoons chopped watercress leaves for garnish

1. In a small saucepan, bring water to a boil. Blanch the garlic for 2 minutes. Drain.

2. In the bowl of a food processor fitted with the metal blade, add the blanched garlic and shallots and process until finely minced. Add the watercress and continue pulsing. Add the mustard and sour cream and pulse to form a thick paste. Add the lemon juice, salt, and pepper. Pulse a few more times to mix well. Place in a medium saucepan and set aside.

3. Cut the smoked chicken into ¼-inch strips. Set aside.

4. In a large stockpot, bring lightly salted water to a boil and cook the pasta to al dente. Drain, place in a large pasta bowl, and toss with 1 teaspoon of the butter and salt and pepper to taste. Keep warm.

5. Meanwhile, add the remaining 1 teaspoon butter to a small nonstick skillet. Add the chicken breast strips and watercress sauce and warm over medium heat. Toss into the pasta, mix well, and serve sprinkled with the chopped watercress in 4 warmed bowls.

Serves 4

Nutritional Breakdown: *475 calories, 4.6 g fat—9% calories from fat, 37.1 mg cholesterol, 2.8 g fiber, 1,202 mg sodium*

HEARTY CORN, CHICKEN, AND CHILE SOUP

If you're expecting guests, double this recipe to make a big pot of wonderfully flavored low-fat soup.

2 ears husked corn
2 teaspoons olive oil
2 teaspoons canola or other vegetable oil
4 skinless, boneless chicken breast halves (about 1½ pounds), cut into strips
1 tablespoon cornmeal
¼ teaspoon salt
¼ teaspoon freshly ground white pepper
1 teaspoon ground cumin
1 cup chopped green bell pepper
¼ cup chopped red bell pepper
1 cup chopped green onion, white and green parts
2 cups Defatted Chicken Stock (see page 18)
¼ cup drained and chopped canned green chilies
1 cup low-fat buttermilk
2 tablespoons chopped fresh cilantro

1. Fire up the grill. Rub each ear of corn with 1 teaspoon of olive oil. Grill 4 to 6 inches from the hot coals, turning frequently, for 12 minutes, or until done. Cut corn kernels from husks. Set aside.

2. In a large nonstick skillet or sauté pan, heat the oil. Add the chicken breast strips and cook just until brown, about 2 minutes. Remove and set aside.

3. Sprinkle the cornmeal, salt, pepper, cumin, and red and green bell peppers into the skillet. Cook over medium-high heat, stirring constantly, until the bell peppers are partially cooked, about 2 minutes. Add the corn kernels and green onion and stir constantly for 1 minute more.

4. To the skillet, add 1 cup of the chicken stock and cook over medium heat, stirring constantly, until the liquid reduces slightly, about 4 minutes. Add the green chilies, chicken strips, the remaining 1 cup stock, and the buttermilk. Over very low heat, cook, partially covered, for 5 minutes more, until the chicken is done. Divide among 4 bowls, and sprinkle with the chopped cilantro.

Serves 4

Nutritional Breakdown: *373 calories, 8.9 g fat—21% calories from fat, 87.6 mg cholesterol, 4.7 g fiber, 1,642 mg sodium*

SPICY CHICKEN AND 3-BEAN CHILI

Serve with your favorite low-fat or non-fat toppings, such as nonfat sour cream, chopped green onions, reduced-fat Cheddar cheese, and chopped cilantro. This is a thick, chunky, and hearty approach to the usual one-bowl meal we know fondly as chili.

2 tablespoons canola or other vegetable oil
1 large onion, chopped
3 garlic cloves, chopped
2 tablespoons chili powder
¼ teaspoon crushed red pepper, or more to taste
1 pound ground skinless, boneless chicken breast
1 small eggplant, peeled and cut into small cubes
1 large can (16 ounces) black beans, rinsed and drained
1 large can (16 ounces) pinto or red kidney beans, rinsed and drained
1 large can (16 ounces) white great northern beans, rinsed and drained
1 large can (about 16 ounces) Mexican-style whole cooked tomatoes, drained and chopped
1 can (8 ounces) tomato sauce
2 stalks celery, sliced
1 medium green bell pepper, chopped
1 teaspoon ground cumin
Salt and freshly ground black pepper

1. In a heavy, large nonstick skillet, heat the oil over medium heat. Add the chopped onion and garlic and cook about 2 minutes. Add the chili powder and red pepper and stir for 1 minute. Add the ground chicken breast and cook, stirring occasionally, until slightly browned, about 3 minutes. Add the eggplant and cook, stirring occasionally, until almost done, about 5 minutes.

2. To the skillet, add all the beans, tomatoes, tomato sauce, celery, bell pepper, and cumin. Stir to mix well. Bring to a simmer and continue cooking, stirring frequently, for 25 to 30 minutes more. Adjust the seasoning with salt and pepper to taste.

3. Serve hot in 4 large low bowls. Sprinkle on the desired toppings.

Serves 4

Nutritional Breakdown: *589 calories, 10.7 g fat—16% calories from fat, 65.7 mg cholesterol, 18.1 g fiber, 1,481 mg sodium*

COLD CHICKEN BREASTS WITH PINEAPPLE RELISH

Instead of pineapple, use several other fruits, such as cantaloupe, grapes, mangoes, and papayas. Why not make a "fruit salad" relish with a mix of fresh fruits?

4 skinless, boneless chicken breasts (about 1½ pounds), trimmed and pounded between plastic wrap to ¼-inch thick
Salt and freshly ground white pepper
2 tablespoons vermouth or dry white wine
¼ cup Rich Chicken Stock (see page 16)
2 teaspoons finely minced garlic
1½ tablespoons grated peeled fresh ginger
1 tablespoon toasted and ground mustard seed, or 1 teaspoon dry mustard
3 tablespoons packed light brown sugar
3 cups chopped fresh pineapple with 3 tablespoons juice
3 tablespoons sherry vinegar

1. Place the chicken breasts in a large glass baking dish. Lightly season with salt and pepper. In a cup, combine the vermouth, chicken stock, and garlic. Drizzle over the chicken and marinate for 30 minutes, covered tightly with plastic wrap. Drain and reserve the marinade.

2. Lightly coat a cast-iron stove-top grilling pan or large skillet with cooking spray. Heat to very hot and cook the breasts for 2 to 3 minutes per side, until done. Do not overcook. Place the chicken on a platter, cover with plastic wrap, and chill.

3. In a heavy skillet, combine the reserved marinade, ginger, mustard seed, sugar, pineapple juice, and vinegar. Cook over medium-high heat until reduced by about two thirds, about 5 minutes. Add the pineapple and continue cooking for 10 minutes more, or until almost all the liquid is evaporated and just pineapple and syrup remain in the pan. Chill and serve beside the chicken.

Serves 4

Nutritional Breakdown: *319 calories, 3.6 g fat—10% calories from fat, 98.7 mg cholesterol, 1.6 g fiber, 204 mg sodium*

CHICKEN AND ROASTED ARTICHOKE RISOTTO

6 cups Defatted Chicken Stock (see page 18)
¾ pound baby artichokes (about 8)
8 garlic cloves, peeled
2 teaspoons fresh thyme leaves
2 tablespoons plus 1 teaspoon extra-virgin olive oil
Salt and freshly ground black pepper
2 skinless, boneless chicken breast halves (about ¾ pound)
3 tablespoons finely chopped prosciutto
1 teaspoon dried thyme
1 tablespoon unsalted butter
2 tablespoons finely minced shallots
1½ cups arborio rice
1 cup dry white wine
3 tablespoons finely grated aged Parmesan

1. Preheat the oven to 375° F.
2. In a medium saucepan, simmer the chicken stock until reduced by one third, about 10 minutes. Set aside.
3. To prepare the artichokes, rinse the artichokes well. Trim off the tough part of the stem and the tops of the leaves. Snap off the tough outer leaves. Arrange the artichokes close together in a glass baking dish. Push the garlic cloves in between the artichokes. Sprinkle on the 2 teaspoons thyme leaves and drizzle on 1 tablespoon of the oil. Season lightly with salt and pepper. Cover tightly with foil and bake for 45 minutes. Remove the foil and return to the oven for 10 minutes more. Remove the garlic cloves and discard. Coarsely chop the artichokes. Set aside.
4. Meanwhile, in a large nonstick skillet, heat 1 tablespoon of the oil. Season the chicken breasts with salt and pepper, and cook over moderately high heat, turning frequently, until browned on both sides, about 3 minutes per side. Shred the chicken into strips and set aside.
5. In a small nonstick saucepan, cook the prosciutto over medium-high heat until crispy. Set on paper towels to drain. Pat off any excess oil.
6. In a medium saucepan, warm the reduced chicken stock and keep warm over very low heat. Add the 1 teaspoon dried thyme to the stock.
7. In a large heavy saucepan, heat the remaining 1 teaspoon of oil and the butter. Add the shallots and cook for 3 minutes, or just until translucent. Add the rice and stir to coat with the oil, about

1 minute. Add 1 cup of warm chicken stock and cook over medium heat, stirring constantly until the moisture is almost absorbed into the rice. Continue adding all the stock, ¾ cup at a time, stirring constantly, until the liquid is almost absorbed before adding more, and the mixture is creamy. In the last addition, add the wine with the stock, and stir in the chicken and chopped artichoke.

8. When the mixture is creamy, the liquid is absorbed, and the rice is done to al dente (after about 25 minutes), remove the pan from the heat. Stir in the Parmesan and divide among 4 preheated shallow pasta bowls. Serve immediately.

Serves 4

Nutritional Breakdown: *699 calories, 17.6 g fat—23% calories from fat, 84.8 mg cholesterol, 4.8 g fiber, 2,562 mg sodium*

PAN-SEARED CHICKEN BREASTS WITH BASIL SAUCE

1½ teaspoons unsalted butter
1½ teaspoons extra-virgin olive oil
4 skinless, boneless chicken breast halves (about 1½ pounds), pounded between plastic wrap to ⅓ inch thick
½ cup Chardonnay or other dry white wine
2 shallots, finely minced
1 medium garlic clove, finely minced
1¼ cups finely chopped fresh basil
4 tablespoons finely chopped flat-leaf parsley
¼ cup Rich Chicken Stock (see page 16)
½ cup low-fat milk
½ teaspoon fresh lemon juice
Salt and freshly ground white pepper

1. In a large nonstick skillet lightly coated with cooking spray, heat the butter and oil. When the pan is very hot, sear the chicken breasts for 2 to 3 minutes per side, or just until done. Transfer to a platter. Cover with foil to keep warm.

2. Deglaze the pan with ¼ cup of the wine, scraping the bottom to loosen the brown bits. Add the shallots and garlic and cook over high heat for 1 minute. Add the basil, 3 tablespoons of the parsley, the remaining wine, the chicken stock, milk, and lemon juice and cook over medium heat, stirring constantly, until the mixture is reduced by half.

Adjust the seasoning with salt and pepper to taste.

3. Place sauce in the center of 4 preheated serving plates and place a chicken breast in the sauce. Sprinkle with the remaining tablespoon of parsley.

Serves 4

Nutritional Breakdown: *329 calories, 6.5 g fat—18% calories from fat, 137 mg cholesterol, 0.5 g fiber, 257 mg sodium*

CREOLE-STYLE CHICKEN GUMBO

1 tablespoon canola or other vegetable oil
1 cup finely chopped yellow onion
1 cup finely chopped celery
2 large garlic cloves, finely minced
1 large green bell pepper, finely chopped
4 skinless, boneless chicken breast halves (about 1½ pounds), cut in quarters
4 ounces andouille (spicy) sausage, chopped
1 cup Defatted Chicken Stock (see page 18)
1 can (14 ounces) tomatoes in puree
1 teaspoon Tabasco sauce, or more to taste
⅛ teaspoon cayenne
¼ cup chopped flat-leaf parsley
2 teaspoons chopped fresh thyme, or 1 teaspoon dried
½ teaspoon freshly ground black pepper
2 teaspoons Louisiana gumbo seasoning
1 tablespoon tomato paste
4 cups or more freshly cooked white rice, hot

1. In a large nonstick skillet lightly coated with cooking spray, heat the oil. Add the onion, celery, garlic, and bell pepper and cook, stirring, until the onion is translucent, about 5 minutes.

2. To the skillet, add the chicken pieces and cook over medium heat until lightly browned, about 6 minutes. Add the sausage and cook for 3 minutes more.

3. To the skillet, add the chicken stock, tomatoes in puree, Tabasco sauce, cayenne, parsley, thyme, black pepper, gumbo seasoning, and tomato paste. Stir well. Bring the sauce to a boil, reduce the heat to a simmer, and cook until the chicken is done, about 6 to 8 minutes. Adjust the seasoning with salt and Tabasco. Serve over the hot rice.

Serves 4 to 6

Nutritional Breakdown: *653 calories, 16.1 g fat—23% calories from fat, 143 mg cholesterol, 4 g fiber, 1,130 mg sodium*

CHICKEN AND FARM-STAND VEGETABLE SOUP

This eggplant soup was inspired by Yvonne Doone, a private chef in Los Angeles.

9½ cups Rich Chicken Stock (see page 16)
1 garlic clove, peeled
1 large leek, quartered lengthwise and cut into matchsticks
2 parsnips, peeled and sliced
2 stalks celery, thinly sliced
4 small carrots, peeled and halved
4 new potatoes, scrubbed and quartered
4 small or baby turnips, peeled and halved
¼ cup dry white wine
2 skinless, boneless chicken breast halves (about ¾ pound), cut into thin strips
2 large mushrooms, stemmed and thinly sliced
2 tablespoons chopped flat-leaf parsley or fresh dill
1 cup cooked wide egg noodles, hot

1. In a large stockpot, boil 8 cups of the chicken stock and garlic clove, and reduce by one quarter, about 10 minutes. Add the leek, reduce the heat to very low, and simmer, partially covered, for 10 minutes.

2. In a vegetable steamer over simmering water, steam the parsnips, celery, carrots, potatoes, and turnips for 2 minutes. Do not overcook. Transfer to the stock. Cook for 20 minutes or until the vegetables are tender, skimming off any scum that forms on the top during cooking.

3. Meanwhile, in a medium high-sided skillet, heat the remaining stock and the wine to a simmer. Poach the chicken strips just until done, about 5 minutes. Transfer to a strainer and rinse under cold running water to remove scum. Set chicken aside. Do not add this poaching liquid to the vegetables and soup or it will turn cloudy.

4. Remove the garlic from the stock. Add the mushrooms, chicken strips, and chopped parsley or dill. Over low heat, heat the chicken and ingredients through. Divide the noodles among 4 bowls, ladle on the hot soup (stock part only), and distribute the vegetables and chicken strips evenly. Serve hot.

Serves 4 to 6

Nutritional Breakdown: *303 calories, 3.6 g fat—11% calories from fat, 41.7 mg cholesterol, 6.3 g fiber, 1,338 mg sodium*

WHITE WINE COQ AU VIN

16–20 tiny white pearl onions
1 thick slice country bacon, chopped
1 teaspoon extra-virgin olive oil
4 skinless, boneless chicken breast halves (about 1½ pounds), cut into 2-inch pieces
2 cups Rich Chicken Stock (see page 16)
1 cup fruity white wine (such as Chablis)
2 teaspoons chopped fresh thyme, or 1 teaspoon dried
5 tablespoons chopped flat-leaf parsley
3 bay leaves
1 tablespoon chopped fresh marjoram, or 1½ teaspoons dried
2 garlic cloves, minced
½ teaspoon freshly ground white pepper
½ pound mushrooms, trimmed and halved
1¼ cups nonfat sour cream
1 tablespoon cornstarch, dissolved in 2 tablespoons cold water
3 cups cooked egg noodles tossed with 1 teaspoon melted butter, hot

1. In a medium saucepan bring water to a boil. Add the pearl onions and boil for 2 minutes. Cool, trim the root end, and peel, leaving the onion whole.
2. In a large nonstick skillet over high heat, cook the bacon until crispy. Drain on a paper towel and set aside. Pour the fat out but do not wipe the skillet.
3. In the same skillet, heat the oil. Add the chicken breast pieces and cook over medium-high heat just until lightly browned, about 3 to 5 minutes. Remove with a slotted spoon. Set aside.
4. To the skillet, add the stock, wine, thyme, 4 tablespoons of the parsley, the bay leaves, marjoram, garlic, and pepper and bring to a boil. Reduce the heat to a simmer and continue cooking for 12 minutes, or until reduced by one third.
5. Add the onions and mushrooms to the pan and simmer for 5 minutes. Increase the heat to medium and reduce the sauce until 2 cups remain, about 8 to 10 minutes. Stir in the sour cream.
6. Stir in the cornstarch mixture and cook until the sauce thickens, about 1 to 2 minutes. Remove the bay leaves. Add the reserved chicken and bacon and simmer until the chicken is done, about 4 minutes.
7. Serve with the noodles, and sprinkle on the 1 tablespoon chopped parsley.

Serves 4 to 6

Nutritional Breakdown: *371 calories, 5.4 g fat—13% calories from fat, 103 mg cholesterol, 2.2 g fiber, 1,141 mg sodium*

CHICKEN AND SUMMER VEGETABLES WITH PAN-FRIED POLENTA

To save time, look for already prepared polenta in the supermarket, which can be pan-fried on a nonstick surface lightly coated with cooking spray.

4 1½ by 1-inch-thick polenta cakes
4 skinless, boneless chicken breast halves (about 1½ pounds), cut into quarters
Salt and freshly ground black pepper
1 tablespoon canola or other vegetable oil
1 medium onion, coarsely chopped
2 stalks celery, cut on the diagonal
1 green bell pepper, seeded and sliced
1 large zucchini, cut on the diagonal
3 cups Rich Chicken Stock (see page 16)
2 cups peeled, seeded, and coarsely chopped plum tomatoes
2 tablespoons tomato paste
1 garlic clove, finely minced
1 teaspoon crushed red pepper
1 tablespoon fresh lemon juice
2 tablespoons red wine vinegar
4 tablespoons chopped flat-leaf parsley

1. In a large skillet generously coated with cooking spray brown the polenta cakes over medium-high heat. Set in the oven to keep warm.

2. Season the chicken pieces with salt and pepper. In a large nonstick skillet, heat the oil. Add the chicken and cook over medium-high heat until lightly browned on both sides, about 3 to 4 minutes. Transfer the chicken to a bowl. Set aside.

3. To the skillet, add the onion, celery, bell pepper, and zucchini and cook, stirring constantly, until the onion is translucent, about 5 minutes. Add ¼ cup of the chicken stock, partially cover, and continue cooking until the vegetables are tender, about 5 minutes. Transfer to a bowl. Set aside.

4. To the skillet, add the tomatoes, tomato paste, the remaining 2¾ cups stock, the garlic, red pepper, lemon juice, and vinegar. Bring to a boil and reduce by half. Add the chicken pieces and reduce the heat to a simmer, stirring occasionally, until the chicken pieces are done and the liquid is reduced to a sauce, about 5 minutes.

5. Add the reserved vegetables and heat through. Adjust the seasoning with salt and pepper. Add 2 tablespoons of the parsley and stir just to mix. Divide among 4 shallow pasta bowls, sprinkle with the remaining 2 tablespoons parsley, and serve with hot polenta cakes on the side.

Serves 4

Nutritional Breakdown: *327 calories, 7.9 g fat—22% calories from fat, 100 mg cholesterol, 3.1 g fiber, 1,270 mg sodium*

HERBED CHICKEN FRICASSEE

Lots of garlic and fresh herbs recall a hearty stew, cooked Dutch oven style. Serve with a light red wine, such as Dolcetto or Pinot Noir. You'll appreciate the taste of free-range chicken in this case, even though these breasts are a bit more expensive than regular fryers.

3 large garlic cloves
⅔ cup chopped fresh herbs of choice (such as marjoram, thyme, sage, rosemary, and savory)
3 tablespoons red wine vinegar
2 tablespoons exta-virgin olive oil
4 skinless, boneless chicken breast halves (about 1½ pounds), cut into 1½-inch pieces
Salt and freshly ground black pepper
1 small red onion, thinly sliced
1 small white onion, thinly sliced
2 tablespoons all-purpose flour
2 cups dry white wine
2 cups Rich Chicken Stock (see page 16)
16 baby carrots, peeled and trimmed
16 baby zucchini, trimmed
16 baby turnips, scrubbed and trimmed
16 tiny potatoes (such as purple, Yukon gold, and fingerling), scrubbed
1 tablespoon unsalted butter
¼ cup finely chopped parsley

1. In the bowl of a food processor fitted with the metal blade, combine the garlic and fresh herbs, and process to a paste. With the motor running, add the vinegar and 1 tablespoon of the oil in a thin stream, and process until smooth.
2. Place the chicken in a shallow glass baking dish. Coat with the herb mixture, cover tightly with plastic wrap, and marinate for 1 to 3 hours in the refrigerator.

3. Scrape the herb marinade off the chicken and reserve. Season the chicken with salt and pepper. In a large nonstick high-sided skillet or Dutch oven, add the remaining 1 tablespoon oil. Add the chicken and cook over medium-high heat until brown and done throughout, about 10 to 12 minutes. Remove from the skillet and keep warm.

4. In the same skillet, add both onions and cook over medium heat, partially covered, until tender, about 5 minutes. Remove from the skillet and set aside. Put the flour in a small bowl. Add enough wine just to make a thin paste. Add the remaining wine to the same skillet and, over medium heat, stir in the flour paste. Cook, stirring constantly, until reduced by half, about 8 to 10 minutes Scrape the sides and bottom of the pan frequently to loosen any brown bits.

5. Add the reserved herb marinade. Pour the chicken stock into the skillet and cook over high heat until the sauce is reduced by one third, about 8 minutes. Strain and reserve, discarding the cooked herbs. The sauce should equal about 2 cups.

6. In a vegetable steamer over simmering water, steam all the vegetables just until crisp-tender, about 2 minutes. Steam the potatoes until tender, about 5 to 7 minutes. Do not overcook. Set aside.

7. In a large skillet, melt the butter. Add all the steamed vegetables and heat through. Season with salt and pepper to taste. Transfer to a bowl and cover with foil to keep warm. To the same skillet, add the reserved onions, chicken, and sauce. Warm thoroughly over low heat.

8. Place the chicken in the center of a platter. Arrange the vegetables around it, drizzle 1 cup of the sauce over the chicken, and sprinkle with the parsley. Pass the remaining sauce in a bowl, if desired.

Serves 4 to 6

Nutritional Breakdown (includes 1/4 cup of sauce per serving): *739 calories, 13.9 g fat—17% calories from fat, 107 mg cholesterol, 11.5 g fiber, 873 mg sodium*

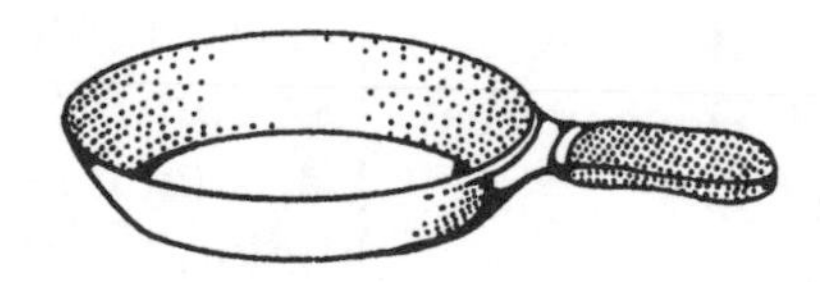

CHICKEN BRAISED IN APPLE JUICE AND FRESH SAGE

Serve this with a nutty-flavored wild rice to perfectly complement this strongly sage-flavored sauce. Make sure fresh sage is available before beginning this recipe.

1½ cups clear apple juice
4 skinless, boneless chicken breast halves (about 1½ pounds)
Salt and freshly ground black pepper
1 teaspoon unsalted butter
1 teaspoon extra-virgin olive oil
1 large garlic clove, minced
1 medium onion, halved and sliced
1 cup dry white wine
1 Bosc pear, peeled, cored, and diced
1½ teaspoons chopped fresh sage
2 ripe plum tomatoes, peeled, seeded, and finely diced
½ cup low-fat or nonfat sour cream
4 sage leaves for garnish

1. Reduce the apple juice in a saucepan over medium-high heat by one third, about 5 minutes.
2. Season the chicken breasts with salt and pepper. In a medium high-sided nonstick skillet lightly coated with cooking spray, heat the butter and oil. Add the garlic and onion and cook over medium heat, stirring constantly, for 2 minutes. Add the chicken breasts and cook just until slightly browned, about 3 minutes per side.
3. Pour in the reduced apple juice and the wine and bring to a boil. Add the pear and sage, reduce the heat to a simmer, and cook, partially covered, until the chicken is done, about 10 to 12 minutes. Remove the chicken breasts to a platter and cover with foil to keep warm.
4. Increase the heat and reduce the sauce to about ⅔ cup, about 5 minutes. Remove the pan from the heat and add the tomatoes and sour cream. Stir and return to low heat, just to heat through. Adjust the seasoning with salt and pepper to taste. Place the breasts on a platter, garnish with the sage leaves, and spoon on the sauce.

Serves 4

Nutritional Breakdown: *348 calories, 4.6 g fat—12% calories from fat, 101 mg cholesterol, 1,8 g fiber, 140 mg sodium*

Index

Asian Chicken, Potato, and Avocado Salad, 28
Asian Orange-Glazed Chicken Breasts, 137

Baked Chicken-Stuffed Zucchini, 57
Baking and roasting, 51–72
Balsamic Chicken Breasts with Vegetables en Papillote, 67
Balsamic Chicken Skewers, 141
Barley Risotto with Chicken and Vegetables, 147
Basil Chicken and Pasta Salad, 30
Blackened Cajun Chicken, 131
Broiling, 119, 140

Caribbean Grilled Chicken, 127
Caribe-Style Chicken Breasts, 140
Champagne and Chanterelle Chicken Breasts, 88
Cheese and Mushroom Quesadillas with Salsa and Creamy Guacamole, 64
Chicken and Asparagus Stir-fry, 102
Chicken and Farm-Stand Vegetable Soup, 168
Chicken and Fennel Salad with Thyme-Mustard Dressing, 50
Chicken and Melon Stir-fry, 103
Chicken and Portobello Mushroom Salad, 111
Chicken and Roasted Artichoke Risotto, 165
Chicken and Snow Pea Rice Salad, 104
Chicken and Summer Vegetables with Pan-fried Polenta, 170
Chicken Braised in Apple Juice and Fresh Sage, 173
Chicken Breasts with Chinese Black Bean Puree, 112
Chicken Breasts with Creamy Spring Onion Sauce, 75
Chicken Breasts with Fruit Salsa, 117
Chicken Breasts with Roasted Onion Marmalade, 136
Chicken Breasts with Tomato and Basil Sauce on Linguine, 79
Chicken Cakes with Balsamic-Shallot Sauce, 76
Chicken in Red Wine Sauce with Pappardelle Pasta, 149
Chicken Niçoise Salad, 80
Chicken Paillards with Mushrooms and Peppers, 77
Chicken Paillards with Walnuts and Parsley Sauce, 93
Chicken, Peas, and Pasta, 159
Chicken Pot Pie with a Potato Top, 54
Chicken, Rice, and Spinach Filled Cabbage Rolls, 56
Chicken-Vegetable Stir-fry, 98
Chicken with Basil, Endive, and Peppers, 91
Chicken with Fig and Port Wine Sauce, 125
Chicken with Grapefruit, Red Onion, and Radicchio, 89
Chicken with Mustard-Cream Sauce, 66
Chilled Chicken Breasts with Cucumber-Dill Sauce, 36
Classic Rosemary Chicken Salad, 94
Cold Chicken Breasts with Pineapple Relish, 164
Couscous, 143
Creole-Chicken Gumbo, 167
Crispy Chicken Cutlets on Garlic Mashed Potatoes, 144
Crispy Ginger Chicken with Sake Dipping Sauce, 138
Crispy Oven-Fried Chicken Breasts, 70
Curried Chicken with Carrot and Onion, 158

Dallas-style Barbecued Chicken, 134

Escalopes of Chicken on Spinach with Lemon and Shallot Sauce, 154

Fig/grape leaves, 55
Free-range chickens, 65
Fusilli with Chicken, Herbs, and Oven-Dried Tomatoes, 120

Ginger-Soy Shredded Chicken Salad, 43
Glazed Chicken Breasts with Peach Chutney, 90
Glazed Chicken Loaf, 61
Goat Cheese and Basil Stuffed Chicken Breasts, 84
Grilled Chicken Burgers with Tomato Chutney, 126
Grilled Chicken with Papaya and Mango Relish, 130
Grilled Rosemary Chicken, Asparagus, and Red Onion Salad, 122
Grilling, 119–31, 123, 134, 142

Hearty Corn, Chicken, and Chile Soup, 162
Herb and Mustard Baked Chicken with Fava Beans, 58
Herbed Chicken Fricassee, 171
Herbed Chicken Salad with Tomato Tabbouleh, 46
Honey-Mustard Chicken with Mushroom Ragout, 156

Japanese Stir-fry with Peas, 96

Layered Chicken Enchiladas, 68
Lemon-Thyme Chicken Breasts, 87
Lemony Artichoke, Parmesan, and Chicken Salad, 44

Mango Chutney Chicken, 29
Marinades, 129, 143
Mediterranean Chicken and Green Bean Salad, 45

Oils, 78, 97
Olive and Feta Stuffed Chicken Rolls, 71
Onion Marmalade, 136
Orange Chicken and Peppers with Curly Noodles, 101
Oregano Chicken with Herbed Tomatoes, 27

Pan-Seared Chicken Breasts with Basil Sauce, 166
Paprika Chicken with Egg Noodles, 62
Peanut and Sesame Chicken Salad, 118
Pesto, 155
Pineapple and Chicken Salad with Peanuts, 32
Pizza with the Works!, 60
Plum-Basted Chicken Breasts on Thyme Couscous, 143
Poached Chicken Breasts Pesto, 41
Poached Chicken Breasts with Bean Ragout, 48
Poaching, 25–50
Pot Stickers with Chinese Dipping Sauce, 152

Roasted Chicken, Arugula, and Basil Salad, 53

Sake Sauce, 138
Salsa, 160
Sautéed Chicken Breasts with 20 Shallots, 86
Sautéed Chicken Breasts with Fruity Coconut-Curry Sauce, 83
Sautéed Chicken with Tarragon-Tomato Sauce, 82
Sautéing, 73–94
Shredded Chicken and Wild Rice Salad Lettuce Leaves, 33
Smoked Chicken Breasts and Chopped Sweet Onion Salad, 145
Smoked Chicken Salad with Golden Caviar Sauce, 139
Smoked Chicken Salad with Horseradish Sauce and Apple Slaw, 132
Smoked Chicken with Watercress Sauce over Pasta, 161
Smoking, 119, 121, 133
Soft Tacos Filled with Grilled Chicken and Vegetables, 142
Southwestern Chicken Hash with Spicy Salsa, 160
Soy and Lime Chicken Breasts Steamed in Sake, 116
Spicy Chicken and 3-Bean Chili, 163
Spicy Gazpacho with Chicken and Avocado, 124
Spicy Mexican Grilled Chicken Breasts with Sweet and Hot Citrus Vinaigrette, 128
Spicy Szechwan Baked Chicken, 63
Spinach Pasta with Chicken and Lentils, 148
Steamed Chicken Breast and Zucchini Bundles, 109
Steamed Lemon Chicken Breast Bundles, 107
Steaming, 106–18
Stir-fried Chicken Breasts with Cabbage and Water Chestnuts, 99
Stir-frying, 95–105
Stove top, 146–73
Stuffed Chicken Rolls and Yellow Pepper Sauce, 114
Summer Rolls with Spicy Mint Dipping Sauce, 34
Sweet and Sour Chicken Stir-fry, 100

Tarragon Chicken Breasts with Artichokes, 72
Tequila-Marinated Chicken Ceviche Salad, 42
Thai Chicken Breast Stir-fry, 97
Thai Chicken Satay with Peanut Dipping Sauce, 135
Tomato and Garlic Chicken with Wild Rice, 151

Vietnamese Shredded Chicken and Cabbage Salad, 31

White Wine Coq au Vin, 169
Wine, 153

EQUIVALENT IMPERIAL AND METRIC MEASUREMENTS

American cooks use standard containers, the 8-ounce cup and a tablespoon that takes exactly 16 level fillings to fill that cup level. Measuring by cup makes it very difficult to give weight equivalents, as a cup of densely packed butter will weigh considerably more than a cup of flour. The easiest way therefore to deal with cup measurements in recipes is to take the amount by volume rather than by weight. Thus the equation reads:

1 cup = 240 ml = 8 fl. oz. ½ cup = 120 ml = 4 fl. oz.

It is possible to buy a set of American cup measures in major stores around the world.

In the United States, butter is often measured in sticks. One stick is the equivalent of 8 tablespoons. One tablespoon of butter is therefore the equivalent to ½ ounce/15 grams.

Liquid Measures

Fluid ounces	U.S.	Imperial	Milliliters
	1 teaspoon	1 teaspoon	5
¼	2 teaspoon	1 dessert spoon	7
½	1 tablespoon	1 tablespoon	15
1	2 tablespoon	2 tablespoon	28
2	¼ cup	4 tablespoon	56
4	½ cup or ¼ pint		110
5		¼ pint or 1 gill	140
6	¾ cup		170
8	1 cup or ½ pint		225
9			250, ¼ liter
10	1¼ cups	½ pint	280
12	1½ cups	¾ pint	340
15	¾ pint		420
16	2 cups or 1 pint		450
18	2¼ cups		500, ½ liter
20	2½ cups	1 pint	560
24	3 cups		675 or 1½ pints
25		1¼ pints	700
27	3½ cups		750
30	3¾ cups	1½ pints	840
32	4 cups or 2 pints or 1 quart		900
35		1¾ pints	980
36	4½ cups		1000, 1 liter
40	5 cups or 2½ pints	2 pints or 1 quart	1120
48	6 cups or 3 pints		1350
50		2½ pints	1400
60	7½ cups	3 pints	1680
64	8 cups or 4 pints or 2 quarts		1800
72	9 cups		2000, 2 liters

Solid Measures

U.S. and Imperial Measures		Metric Measures	
ounces	pounds	grams	kilos
1		28	
2		56	
3½		100	
4	¼	112	
5		140	
6		168	
8	½	225	
9		250	¼
12	¾	340	
16	1	450	
18		500	½
20	1¼	560	
24	1½	675	
27		750	¾
28	1¾	780	
32	2	900	
36	2¼	1000	1
40	2½	1100	
48	3	1350	
54		1500	1½
64	4	1800	
72	4½	2000	2
80	5	2250	2¼
90		2500	2½
100	6	2800	2¾

Oven Temperature Equivalents

Fahrenheit	Celsius	Gas Mark	Description
225	110	¼	Cool
250	130	½	
275	140	1	Very Slow
300	150	2	
325	170	3	Slow
350	180	4	Moderate
375	190	5	
400	200	6	Moderately Hot
425	220	7	Fairly Hot
450	230	8	Hot
475	240	9	Very Hot
500	250	10	Extremely Hot

Linear and Area Measures

1 inch	2.54 centimeters
1 foot	0.3048 meters
1 square inch	6.4516 square centimeters
1 square foot	929.03 square centimeters